THE CONSTITUTION
and
ITS AMENDMENTS

THE CONSTITUTION
and
ITS AMENDMENTS

Volume 1

Roger K. Newman
Editor in Chief

MACMILLAN REFERENCE USA
NEW YORK

Copyright © 1999 by Macmillan Reference USA

Macmillan Reference USA
1633 Broadway
New York, NY 10019

Library of Congress Catalog Card Number: 98-8570

Printed in the United States of America

Printing Number
3 4 5 6 7 8 9 10

Library of Congress Cataloging-in-Publication Data
The constitution and its amendments/ Roger K. Newman, editor in chief.

     p.   cm.
   Includes index.
   ISBN 0-02-864858-7 (set : alk. paper).—ISBN 0-02-864854-4
   (Vol.1 : alk. paper). ISBN 0-02-864855-2 (Vol. 2 : alk. paper)
   1. Constitutional amendments–United States–History.
   I. Newman, Roger K.
 KF4557. C66   1998
 342.73'03–98-8570 CIP dc21

This paper meets the requirements of ANSI-NISO Z39.48-1992 (Permanence of Paper).

CONTENTS

VOLUME 1

VOLUME 2

VOLUME 3

VOLUME 4

Preface

Interest in law in the United States has never been stronger or more intense than it is today. In our entertainment, our daily news, our politics, law surrounds us. A common commitment to our highest law—the Constitution—is one of the few bonds that ties all Americans together. Yet there is no one single comprehensive reference work available to the younger student. *The Constitution and Its Amendments* fills that void. No other remotely similar work exists.

The Constitution and Its Amendments is a comprehensive, four-volume primer for students learning about the Constitution for the first time in a formal way. It supplements regular course materials. There are 165 articles, organized by constitutional clauses, by 121 authors. While most of the essays discuss specific articles or amendments, some entries focus on certain concepts, on a subject of importance during a particular period, or on essential cases. Entries are no longer than 2,500 words, broken into several sections, and are nearly always chronological. Key terms are defined in the side columns, next to the sentence in which they first appear. Each entry has at least one sidebar and one often humorous illustration. An Index and a Glossary complete the work. The Glossary defines the words and key terms that might not be readily understandable to the younger readers.

Older students as well as the public at large will find that, because of its range and depth, the work addresses their questions in an easily explainable way. It is not an analytical compendium, although it does contain much information that may be helpful to specialists.

Accessibility is the hallmark of a useful reference work. All the articles are written in an easily understandable style, with technical subjects elucidated so that they can be easily grasped. *The Constitution and Its Amendments* treats our most important national document as a working instrument of government and society in a way young people can understand.

The Constitution and Its Amendments was a group effort from the beginning. Elly Dickason, the publisher at Macmillan Library Reference, and Hélène Potter, senior editor, were continually sympathetic, encouraging, and supportive. They made sure that the final product met the highest possible standards. William Cohen and Sanford Levinson, the project's editorial advisors, were most helpful in developing the list of articles and contributors. The contributors come from a pool of experts. They include two Pulitzer Prize winners and winners of numerous other prizes, some of the most eminent names in American academe, law, and journalism. They understand that their mission is to educate the upcoming generation in the history, tradition, and contemporary status of each clause or subject.

I thank them all, for without them this work would not have been possible.

Roger K. Newman

List of Contributors

Adler, David Gray
Idaho State University
The Executive Branch
Pardon Power

Alexander, Larry
University of San Diego
Hate Speech

Amar, Akhil Reed
Yale University
Fourteenth Amendment:
Introduction

Amar, Vikram David
University of California at Davis
Right to a Jury Trial

Anastaplo, George
Loyola University of Chicago
Preamble

Baer, Judith A.
Texas A&M University
Gender Discrimination

Baldwin, Gordon B.
University of Wisconsin at Madison
Republican Form of Government

Barnett, Randy E.
Boston University
Ninth Amendment

Barrett, Edward L., Jr.
Medford, Oregon
Tax and Spend Power

Beale, Sara Sun
Duke University
Grand Jury

Belknap, Michal R.
California Western University
Subversive Speech

Bell, Tom W.
University of Dayton
Third Amendment

Bennett, Robert W.
Northwestern University
Substantive Due Process

Best, Judith A.
State University of New York at Cortland
Twelfth Amendment

Binder, Sarah A.
The Brookings Institution
United States Senate

Birkby, Robert H.
Vanderbilt University
Prior Restraints: *Near v. Minnesota*

Bobbit, Philip
University of Texas at Austin
Supremacy Clause

Bradley, Craig
Indiana University
Unreasonable Searches and Seizures

Calabresi, Steven G.
Northwestern University
Removal of Officers

Carter, T. Barton
Boston University
Regulating the Electronic Mass Media

Chamberlin, Bill F.
University of Florida
Newsgathering

Chemerinsky, Erwin
University of Southern California
Contemporary Judicial Review
Privacy

Choper, Jesse H.
University of California at Berkeley
No "Establishment of Religion"

Cottrol, Robert J.
George Washington University
Armed Forces
Militia
Second Amendment

Curtis, Michael Kent
Wake Forest University
Fourteenth Amendment:
Enactment

Cushman, Barry
St. Louis University
Commerce Clause: The New Deal

Cushman, Mark V.
Johns Hopkins University
Extradition
Fiscal and Monetary Powers

Drechsel, Robert E.
University of Wisconsin at Madison
Access to the Media

Drinan, Robert F.
Georgetown University
House of Representatives

DuBois, Ellen Carol
University of California at Los Angeles
Nineteenth Amendment

Eisenberg, Theodore
Cornell University
Judiciary

Eisgruber, Christopher L.
New York University
Impact of Judicial Review: *Dred Scott v. Sandford*

Ernst, Daniel R.
Georgetown University
Treason

Feerick, John D.
Fordham University
Twenty-fifth Amendment

Fineman, Martha Albertson
Columbia University
The Constitution and the Family

Finkelman, Paul
University of Akron
Slavery and the Constitution

Fisher, Louis
Library of Congress
Commander-in-Chief
War Power

Fishman, Clifford S.
Catholic University of America
Wiretapping and Electronic Surveillance

Flaherty, Martin S.
Fordham University
Enforcing the Laws

Frank, John P.
Phoenix, Arizona
Flag Salute Cases

Friedman, Barry
Vanderbilt University
Writ of Habeas Corpus

Introduction

★ **Constitutional Origins**
Jack Rakove

ratification process of making a document legal by giving it formal approval

Articles of Confederation the first constitution of the thirteen original United States; in effect 1781–1789

O n May 25, 1787, the delegates from seven states gathered at Independence Hall in Philadelphia, and the Constitutional Convention began its work, only eleven days late. The Framers continued to meet throughout the summer until they completed their work. The Convention finally adjourned on September 17, 1787. The new document that they had drafted, the Constitution of the United States, was sent to the states for ratification on September 28, 1787.

The publication of the Constitution launched an impassioned public debate that lasted into the following summer. By late June 1788, ten states had ratified the Constitution, guaranteeing that a new government would replace the one formed under the Articles of Confederation, adopted by the thirteen states during the Revolutionary War. The Constitution went into effect in March 1789. It has remained the fundamental charter of American government ever since.

In drafting the Constitution, the Framers drew upon many sources of wisdom and political experience. They were well read in the classic works of political theory, from those of the ancient Greeks to the writers of the eighteenth-century Enlightenment, the philosophical movement that rejected much established social, religious and political thinking, and emphasized reason. But they also learned from their own political experience. So, when the colonists declared independence from Great Britain in 1776, they began writing new constitutions, both for their separate states and for the national government of the Continental Congress. When the Framers of the Constitution assembled in 1787, the weaknesses and defects of the state constitutions and the Articles of Confederation were their chief concern.

The Articles of Confederation

The Continental Congress first took up the subject of confederation in June 1776, as it was preparing to declare independence. Led by John Dickinson of Pennsylvania, a committee of thirteen members prepared a set of articles of confederation. Their draft was reported to the full Congress in early July 1776 and was thoroughly debated that summer.

The debates over the Articles of Confederation quickly identified three critical sources of disagreement. First, while delegates from the more populous states favored apportioning representation in the unicameral Congress according to population, members from the small states insisted that each state should receive an equal vote. Second, the delegates disagreed over the formula to be used to apportion the expenses of the Revolutionary War among the states. Third, states lacking valid claims to the interior regions proposed that Congress be given authority over these unsettled lands. Delegates from states possessing such claims resisted.

When the delegates could not resolve these disputes, they put the matter of the Confederation aside. In April 1777, discussion of these

apportion divide proportionally or share according to a plan, such as representatives or taxes under a government

unicameral having one chamber

▶ Patrick Henry, a patriot from Virginia, addresses the delegates at the First Continental Congress, urging them to adopt resolutions for putting the colonies in a state of defense against their former ruler.

matters began again but soon bogged down. Not until the fall of 1777 did Congress show its will to complete the Confederation. The delegates settled the representation problem in favor of the small states, adopted an unworkable formula to apportion war expenses according to the value of improved land in each state, and allowed the states with land claims to keep them.

In November 1777, Congress sent the completed Articles of Confederation to the state legislatures, whose unanimous approval was required for ratification. Stubborn opposition from the states without land claims delayed ratification until February 1781, when Maryland, the last holdout, finally gave its approval.

Features of the Confederation

Several features of the Confederation deserve special mention. First, with each state having an equal vote, it was unlikely that the more populous states would entrust great authority to Congress. Second, all effective power was vested in the unicameral Congress. Congress could create executive departments and a limited number of courts, but these were not constitutionally independent. Third, although Congress controlled matters of war and peace, many of its decisions relating to the conduct of war had to be performed by the states. Congress would adopt resolutions and requisitions asking the states to do various things, such as levying taxes, collecting supplies, or raising an army, but the states themselves would determine how to implement those measures. Fourth, amendments to the Articles required the approval of all thirteen state legislatures.

Amending the Articles

By 1781, many delegates believed that Congress needed more authority than the Articles of Confederation gave it. So, early that year, an

vest to grant with particular authority, property, and rights

resolution a formal statement of opinion or determination voted by an official group

requisition the formal act of calling upon a person or state to carry out an action

levy impose or collect a tax

▲ The first American flag.

amendment was sent to the states to allow Congress to collect an impost—a duty on imported goods. But this amendment failed to receive the unanimous approval required. Rhode Island refused to ratify it, and Virginia later repealed its approval.

In April 1783, with the war over and independence secured, Congress proposed new amendments. One amendment called for a revised impost and another amendment to replace the unworkable provision for apportioning common expenses with a simple formula based on population (with slaves being counted as three-fifths of free persons). These amendments also failed to gain the approval of all thirteen states. Two other amendments proposed in 1784, to give Congress limited authority to regulate foreign commerce, suffered the same fate.

Many national leaders found the character of the constitutions adopted by the individual states after independence even more disturbing than the lack of a national power to tax or to regulate. While these constitutions had generally created independent executive and legislative branches of government, most of the real power to govern was given to the legislatures, which often seemed to act impulsively and unwisely. While the legislatures often did their best to support Congress, their failure to approve amendments to the Articles of Confederation led some national leaders to wonder how long they could count on the states for support.

James Madison's Views

Among the nation's leaders, the most thoughtful was James Madison, who had served in Congress from 1780 to 1783 before returning to the legislature of his native Virginia. In January 1786, the Virginia assembly invited the other states to attend a conference to consider an amendment to the Articles of Confederation giving Congress the power to regulate commerce. After some initial doubts, Madison decided this scheme offered one last chance to reverse the flow of power away from Congress.

Meeting at Annapolis. Yet when the date arrived, only a dozen commissioners from five states showed up at the meeting in Annapolis, Maryland—too few to accomplish their goal. Rather than adjourn empty-handed, Madison and his colleagues, who included John Dickinson of Pennsylvania and Alexander Hamilton of New York, proposed that a new meeting be held at Philadelphia in May 1787, and that its agenda include the general condition of the Confederation. Again, Virginia took the lead in inviting the other states to participate. Every state except Rhode Island approved this convention, as did the Continental Congress, even though nothing in the Articles of Confederation suggested that such a meeting could legally be held.

Meeting at Philadelphia. As a member of the Virginia delegation, Madison prepared carefully for the meeting at Philadelphia. He combined his deep knowledge of history and political philosophy with lessons from his own experience in American politics. Madison concluded that the American union of states was founded on a fundamental error: As long as the national government depended on the individual states to

Most delegates to the Convention were young men in their twenties and thirties. James Madison was only 36 in 1787. In 1776 he helped to frame the Virginia Constitution. There he first showed his lifelong commitment to freedom of religion. Madison was a leader in Virginia politics and, as a member of the Confederation Congress in the 1780s, he supported a stronger national government. At first glance he was not impressive; he was short, thin, and soft-spoken. But he was thoughtful and a hard worker. He arrived in Philadelphia a week early so that he would have time to read and organize his thoughts. He had already developed a plan for creating a new national government—the Virginia Plan—which, after much debate, was used as the basis for discussion on improving the government. The Framers had decided to keep their discussions secret, although delegates were free to take notes. Madison attended nearly every session and kept careful notes. He was the only delegate to do so. Much of what we know today about what happened at the Convention is based on his records.

enforce its measures, it would always be weak and go from crisis to crisis. To remedy this flaw, the national government must be allowed to act directly on the people of the United States. It should have the power to enact, carry out, and judge its own laws, while leaving the states free to conduct their own affairs, subject to national review.

The Virginia Plan. Madison believed that such a national government would need to take a new institutional form. In place of the unicameral Continental Congress, he thought that the Constitutional Convention should propose a true government consisting of a **bicameral** legislature and independent executive and judicial departments. Madison drew upon his criticisms of the state constitutions, where the executive and judiciary were independent in theory, but in practice were no match for the politically more powerful legislatures. Madison proposed that both houses of the new Congress should be elected on some principle of proportional representation, since the American union would become something more than a confederation of equal **sovereign** states.

Madison included these ideas in the Virginia Plan, which he and the other members of his state's delegation drafted while they waited for the members from the other states to arrive in Philadelphia. Once the Constitutional Convention got under way, the Virginia Plan set the basic agenda for the delegates' deliberations during the summer of 1787.

The Debates at Philadelphia

Madison's strategy for the Convention rested on another idea as well. As did other leaders from the more populous states, he deeply disliked the Confederation's arrangement that gave each state an equal vote in the Continental Congress. He believed that state representation should be apportioned according to population, with perhaps some weight given to each state's wealth, and that this principle should be applied to both houses of the new national legislature. Along with James Wilson of Pennsylvania, Rufus King of Massachusetts, and Alexander Hamilton, Madison insisted that decisions about the powers of the new government had to wait until this basic question of representation was settled. As a result, the Convention spent nearly seven weeks debating principles of representation before it made real progress on any other issue.

The Legislative Branch. Two crucial decisions emerged from these disputes, which at times seemed capable of breaking up the Convention. The first concerned the House of Representatives, which the delegates quickly agreed should be elected by the people. But delegates from the southern slave-holding states had a special demand. They were worried that a Congress dominated by the northern states might seek to limit or abolish slavery, and they insisted that any acceptable plan for apportioning seats in the House had to include slaves in the formula for representation, even though slaves could never be considered as citizens or voters. The result was the adoption of a provision requiring the national

bicameral having two chambers

sovereign having complete independence in its relations with other nations or units of government

Benjamin Franklin was, at eighty-one, the oldest of the fifty-five delegates to the Constitutional Convention. He was instrumental in framing the compromise between the large and small states on the question of representation in the House of Representatives. When he made this recommendation, he remarked that "when a broad table is to be made, and the edges of the plank do not fit, the artist takes a little from both and makes a good joint." After the final draft of the Constitution was completed, it was suggested that Franklin address the Convention to ask that all the delegates, despite the deep misgivings of some, sign the Constitution. He was in failing health, and his address was read for him. "I agree to this Constitution with all its faults, if they are such," Franklin wrote, "because I think a General Government necessary for us . . . ." The delegates all signed it, and afterward, Franklin remarked to members sitting near him that he was convinced now that the painting of the sun over the presiding officer's chair "is a rising and not a setting sun."

government to take a census every ten years and to count a slave as three-fifths of a free person for purposes of representation.

The second and more difficult issue concerned the Senate. The Constitutional Convention agreed that the state legislatures should elect this upper house, which was meant to provide a prudent check on an impulsive House of Representatives. This decision implied that the purpose of the Senate was to represent the states, but it did not necessarily mean that the states had to keep the equal-vote rule of the Confederation. Nonetheless, delegates from the less populous states insisted that their constituents would never ratify a constitution that took away this privilege. On July 16, 1787, the small states narrowly won this point in a key vote, thus ensuring that each state, regardless of population, would have an equal vote in the Senate.

Madison and his allies regarded this decision as a defeat, and for a brief time they were uncertain whether they should proceed as planned. But having invested so much in the Convention already, they had no alternative but to go on.

The Executive Branch. In late July 1787, the Framers turned their attention to the executive branch. The delegates had earlier agreed that the final responsibility for overseeing the administration of the national government and its laws should fall to one person. Yet nearly everything else about the presidency seemed confusing, especially the way the chief executive should be elected, the term of office he should serve, and whether he should be allowed to seek reelection. The Framers' basic goal was to make the president politically independent of Congress, so that he could carry out his duties free from excessive congressional meddling but still be held responsible for his actions.

Finally, by early September, the Framers were able to agree on the structure of the presidency. The power to elect the president was given to an electoral college, to be chosen within the separate states. If the electors failed to produce a majority for any candidate, the final decision would go to the House of Representatives, voting by states. The president was given a limited veto power over legislation. Late in the deliberations, the power to negotiate treaties and to make appointments, which the Convention originally had granted to the Senate, was transferred to the president, acting with the advice and consent of the upper house.

The Judicial Branch. The Constitutional Convention also established a national judiciary, consisting of a Supreme Court and such other courts as Congress chose to create. The Framers feared that if enforcement of national laws was left solely to state courts, those laws would be easily violated or ignored. To bind state courts to accept national law, the Convention adopted a clause making the Constitution and the laws and treaties of the United States made under its authority "the supreme law of the land." This meant that the federal court system would have the principal authority, on appeal, to enforce the Constitution, certainly against any actions by the states that violated the Constitution but also against questionable actions of Congress.

prudent careful concerning one's own interest

constituent a voter in a district who elects an official for representation

electoral college a body of people chosen by the voters in each state to elect the president and vice president of the United States

supreme having the highest authority

▶ The original American colonies represented as segments of a snake in a historic engraving urging the colonies to unite. Printed by Benjamin Franklin.

Ratification of the Constitution

To make the authority of the Constitution supreme, the Framers proposed a special set of procedures for its ratification. Unlike the Articles of Confederation, which had been approved only by the state legislatures, the Constitution was to be submitted to popularly elected conventions in each state. The Framers feared that if the Constitution was approved by a legislative act only, then future sessions of these state legislatures would have the same legal authority to enact measures interfering with the Constitution. But if a popular convention ratified the Constitution, its authority would flow from a direct expression of the will of the sovereign American people. And to make sure that the American people spoke in a clear voice, the Framers and their supporters, known as Federalists, imposed one other limit on the ratification process. The state conventions would be allowed to vote only for or against the Constitution in its entirety. They could not adopt some parts while rejecting others. And although the state conventions could propose amendments, they could not make their ratification conditional upon the acceptance of any such amendments.

Once the Constitution was published, Federalists rushed it to win speedy victories in five states: Delaware, Georgia, New Jersey, Pennsylvania, and Connecticut. Then difficult obstacles to ratification appeared. The Anti-Federalists, who opposed the Constitution, had condemned its potential for tyranny almost as soon as it was completed. Their main charge was that the Constitution would unite the separate states into one nation, leaving the state governments with few resources and little real business. But the Anti-Federalists found seeds of tyranny in many clauses of the Constitution. Their charges echoed widely in the new nation, where the fear of concentrated government power ran deep.

Anti-Federalist delegates won either clear majorities or near majorities in most of the remaining eight states. To secure ratification, Federalist leaders had to find some formula to quiet their opponents' fears. The solution they generally adopted was to agree to recommend some

Federalist advocating a strong central government of separate states and the adoption of the U.S. Constitution

Anti-Federalist member of the group opposing the adoption of the U.S. Constitution; favored states' rights and argued successfully for the Bill of Rights

tyranny an oppressive government, often where a single ruler has absolute power

★ Constitutional Concepts
Roger K. Newman

supreme having the highest authority

amendments for the first Congress to consider when it was to meet soon after the Constitution was ratified. Some of these amendments took the form of statements affirming basic civil and political rights. Federalists were willing to endorse these amendments even if they privately believed that such declarations were of little use. But they would not accept amendments that proposed changes in the basic structure and powers of the new government.

Using these political tactics, the Federalists managed to get the Constitution ratified after difficult struggles in Massachusetts, New Hampshire, Virginia, and New York. The Constitution was defeated only in Rhode Island and North Carolina. By the summer of 1788, eleven states had ratified the Constitution, and preparations began for the first elections that would enable the new government of the United States to get under way.

The United States Constitution is the supreme law of the land. It establishes the form of the United States government and the rights and liberties of the American people. The Constitution made the United States a nation. It is the very symbol of American unity. And it is under this shield of democracy that Americans continue to govern themselves as a free people.

The Constitution's first words are, "We the people of the United States . . . , do ordain and establish the Constitution for the United States of America." This makes clear that the power of the government comes from the American people. The Constitution created a republic, and the voters elect representatives to govern them.

A Written Constitution

A written constitution provides the basis of government in the United States. It divides powers and duties between the federal and state governments, and it specifies the powers of each branch of the federal government. A written constitution is one of the major contributions the American people have made to the art of government. British royal governors had ruled the colonies under written charters granted by the king. But the idea of adopting a written constitution to embody the basic law of an independent country was entirely new.

One forerunner of the American Constitution was "Agreement of the People." It was conceived by the Levellers, a small band of mid-seventeenth-century English army radicals, and it reads like early drafts of the Constitution and the Bill of Rights. It proposed that a Constitutional Convention draft a written constitution, which would set limits to governmental authority and abolish arbitrary power. England's lack of any written constitution had proved a source of tyranny for the ancestors of many Americans. Thomas Jefferson said about this departure from the English type of government: "Our peculiar security is in the possession of a written Constitution. Let us not make it a blank paper by construction."

"The Blessings of the Constitution." A written document was welcomed as a guarantee against the whims of legislatures.

Why a Written Constitution?

The written Constitution is superior to any law passed by a legislature. The law must agree with the Constitution—as judges interpret it. The overall authority of a written constitution was one of the most influential and radical concepts that came out of the American Revolution. In England the Parliament is all-powerful. The British constitution is unwritten and consists of the whole body of statutes, judicial decisions, practices, and customs that have evolved over centuries; it can be modified simply by an act of Parliament.

Americans in the 1760s and 1770s considered several acts of Parliament governing America to be "unconstitutional." Americans wanted a law that would control the whims of Parliament. From the activity of state legislatures in the 1780s came the idea that written constitutions should serve as a fundamental law that would control legislatures.

The Background of the Constitution

The Framers drew on their past experience as they worked to create a new government. They looked at English history since King John granted the Magna Carta in 1215 and at American history since the first representative assembly met at Jamestown in 1619. But they also learned from the reality of colonial governments that had been established in America for many years. Yet the theory of a limited constitutional government with balanced executive, legislative, and judicial powers was a new one. John

Considered "the Father of the Constitution," James Madison points to the governing document he helped frame.

Adams brought reality and theory together when he wrote the Massachusetts Constitution of 1780, and he became the most eloquent spokesman for the new plan of government at the Constitutional Convention.

"In framing a system which we wish to last for ages," James Madison said at that convention, "we should not lose sight of the changes which ages will provide." The Constitution's principles are in keeping with the beliefs and hopes of a growing democracy. The Framers guaranteed that no majority would have its way unless it could prove itself "persistent and undoubted." They achieved this goal by separating and balancing the powers of government, and by calling for a system of staggered elections, so that not all elected officials would be up for reelection at the same time.

The Constitution has continued to grow in response to the demands of society. Yet its spirit and wording have remained unchanged. Each generation has been able to apply the document's words to its own problems. In 1876 the British statesman William E. Gladstone described the Constitution as "the most wonderful work ever struck off at a given time by the mind and purpose of man."

Principles of American Government

"In framing a government which is to be administered by men over men," Madison wrote in *The Federalist*, No. 51, "the great difficulty lies in this: you must first enable the government to control the governed; and in the next place oblige it to control itself." The Framers were suspicious of people, especially those holding political power. "A hearty Puritanism in the view of human nature . . . pervades the [Constitution]," British statesman James Bryce wrote in 1888. The Framers "believed in original sin, and were resolved to leave open for transgressors no door which they could possibly shut." Yet they wanted a national government strong enough to solve national problems.

The Constitution limits government in various ways. Its principles of separation of powers and of federalism, the "due process" clauses, and the doctrine of judicial review all show the determination to require government to control itself. None of these principles is spelled out in the Constitution. They are either implied in its organization and structure or, as with judicial review, inferred from what Chief Justice John Marshall called "the theory of our government."

Federalism

Federalism provides the framework for American government. It is the division, or sharing, of powers between the national and state governments. The concept has existed since at least 1570, when five Native American groups formed the Iroquois Confederacy, with each tribe having a fixed number of chiefly delegates on a common council. Under the principle of federalism, each government, national or state, is supreme within its own sphere, but neither is supreme within the sphere of the other.

legal tender money which can be legally offered to pay a debt and which the person or institution who is owed the money must accept

THE

FEDERALIST:

ADDRESSED TO THE

PEOPLE OF THE STATE OF NEW-YORK.

NUMBER I.

Introduction.

AFTER an unequivocal experience of the inefficacy of the subsisting federal government, you are called upon to deliberate on a new constitution for the United States of America. The subject speaks its own importance; comprehending in its consequences, nothing less than the existence of the UNION, the safety and welfare of the parts of which it is composed, the fate of an empire, in many respects, the most interesting in the world. It has been frequently remarked, that it seems to have been reserved to the people of this country, by their conduct and example, to decide the important question, whether societies of men are really capable or not, of establishing good government from reflection and choice, or whether they are forever destined to depend, for their political constitutions, on accident and force. If there be any truth in the remark, the crisis, at which we are arrived, may with propriety be regarded as the æra in which

A   that

▲ A page of *The Federalist* inviting the people of the state of New York to ratify the Constitution of the United States.

The national government exercises both enumerated powers (those listed in the constitution) and implied powers (those suggested in the document without being directly stated). Implied powers give the federal government flexibility to expand its powers as conditions change. For example, Congress made paper money legal tender under its expressed powers to borrow money.

All powers not granted to the federal government are reserved for the states. These are called reserved powers. They include conducting elections, providing for public safety (police), creating corporation laws, establishing and maintaining local governments and schools, and making laws about marriage and divorce.

In some areas, the federal and state governments have concurrent powers, and both share authority. These areas include providing for the public welfare, administering criminal justice (courts), chartering banks, and building roads. But where there is a dispute, the national government prevails under the supremacy clause.

Federalism has given Americans a flexible system of government. The national government has the power to act for the nation as a whole. This was necessary during the Great Depression of the early 1930s, for example. At the same time the states have power over important local matters. "It is one of the happy incidents of the federal system," Justice Louis D. Brandeis wrote in a case in 1932, "that a single courageous State may, if its citizens choose, serve as a laboratory, and try novel social and economic experiments without risk to the rest of the country."

Separation of Powers

The Constitution divides the powers of the national (or federal) government among the legislative, executive, and judicial branches.

Article I sets forth the powers of Congress, the legislative branch of government. Congress consists of the Senate and the House of Representatives. Senators are elected for six-year terms while members of the House are elected for two-year terms. Among the powers of Congress are the powers to collect taxes, to regulate commerce, and to declare war.

Article II establishes the executive branch of government headed by the president. It also includes the vice president and any cabinet members and advisers the president appoints. The executive branch is responsible for carrying out the laws that Congress passes. The president is also responsible for foreign relations and is commander in chief of the armed forces.

Article III establishes the judicial branch of government. It calls for a Supreme Court and allows Congress to set up other federal courts. These courts hear cases involving the Constitution and laws Congress passes, as well as cases that involve two or more states.

Checks and Balances

The Constitution sets up a system of checks and balances that allows each branch of government to have a role in the activities of the other two branches. For example, Congress holds a check over the executive branch

veto refuse to sign a bill into law

and the President with its authority to make government appropriations, and it holds a check over the judicial branch with its powers to organize courts and create rules for their procedures. The president can check the legislative branch with his power to veto bills passed in Congress. The courts can check the two other branches by declaring legislative acts and executive orders unconstitutional. This system of checks and balances allows what Madison, in *The Federalist*, No. 51, called the "necessary constitutional means and personal motives to resist the encroachments of the others. . . . Ambition must be made to counteract ambition."

> "We are under a Constitution, but the Constitution is what the judges say it is."
>
> Charles Evans Hughes (1862-1948), Chief Justice, U.S. Supreme Court (1930-1941).

Judicial Review

Judicial review is the method used to answer the basic question: Who is to say what the Constitution means when disputes arise? With judicial review, if the courts find that a law conflicts with the Constitution, that law is declared unconstitutional and cannot be enforced.

The delegates to the Constitutional Convention assumed that the Supreme Court should and would have the power to declare both federal and state legislation unconstitutional. They expected that there would be judicial review, and most delegates were on record as favoring it—but they did not provide for it in the Constitution. The most likely reason is that they believed that the power could be concluded from the wording of the document.

If the Supreme Court did not have this power and if the states had the final say on whether their regulations conformed to federal law, the Union probably would not have held together. State legislatures naturally keep their eye on local problems, and they would probably lose sight of national concerns such as foreign affairs, interstate commerce, and perhaps even civil rights, except as these issues affect those legislators.

An independent judiciary has the primary duty to give force and effect to constitutional liberties as well as to limitations placed upon the legislative and executive branches. By 1835 judicial review became so established that the French commentator Alexis de Tocqueville wrote in *Democracy in America*, "Scarcely any political question arises in the United States that is not resolved, sooner or later, into a judicial question." Judicial review has been called "an attempt by American democracy to cover its bet." It makes the courts the keepers of the constitutional conscience.

The Amendment Process

popular sovereignty government created by and subject to the will of the people

Popular sovereignty allows the people to change the Constitution. Amendments to the Constitution are introduced in Congress. A proposed amendment must have the approval of two-thirds of both houses of Congress. It then goes to the states for their approval. Congress may call a national convention to propose an amendment if two-thirds of the state legislatures approve it. The amendment becomes part of the Constitution only after legislatures or specially chosen conventions in three-fourths of the states have ratified it. Under this method the Bill of Rights was added to the Constitution in 1791.

ratify to formally approve a document, thereby making it legal

President Franklin D. Roosevelt likened his New Deal policies to the process of evolution. The Supreme Court ruled against that legislation in 1935.

Congressmen and senators introduce amendments as easily as they introduce bills. More than 11,000 amendments have been proposed in Congress since 1789. Over three hundred have been introduced to overturn the Supreme Court's 1962 ruling that the government cannot write prayers to be recited in school. About two hundred proposals are usually before Congress at any given time. Yet only twenty-seven amendments, including the Bill of Rights, have been passed since the Constitution itself was ratified. The amendment process is "unwieldy and cumbrous," as Chief Justice Marshall noted.

Interpreting the Constitution

The Constitution is not a code providing for every detail of an unknown future. That would be impossible. To take only two of many examples, wiretapping and the mass media were unknown when the Constitution was drafted. After the Supreme Court in 1935 ruled against the New Deal, President Franklin D. Roosevelt charged that the nation had been relegated to the "horse-and-buggy definition of interstate commerce." Government must be able to act for the public good at any given time. Judicial review allows courts to pass judgment on legislative and executive acts. But on what basis?

How the Constitution should be interpreted is one of the most disputed questions in American history. One approach is "original intent"— that the Constitution should be interpreted according to the intention of those who drafted and adopted it. The history the Framers drew on and the words they used take on enormous significance. Hugo L. Black, who served on the Supreme Court from 1937 to 1971, was the best-known advocate of this approach.

Another approach is the "living Constitution." Woodrow Wilson, before he was president, said, "The Supreme Court is a constitutional convention in continuous session." Under this approach the Constitution is to be kept as up to date as today's news. But the idea that a country's fundamental charter of government should be constantly changing disturbs many people.

The Purpose of the Constitution

The Constitution is rigid in its assertion of personal liberties. These liberties are basic and timeless. They are the very reason that the country was founded. The Constitution is rigid in guaranteeing individual rights; yet it is also a partly adaptable and changing instrument of government. It both creates and limits power at the same time.

The Framers enacted what might be called a "free-enterprise Constitution." After a revolution, they wanted security. They realized that security could best be maintained by providing for government to operate in certain political and economic areas and by prohibiting it from entering others—such as the area of conscience. Although the boundaries of these areas may change over time, their essence does not. As Jefferson said, "The earth belongs to the living, not to the dead." A common commitment to the Constitution is one of the few bonds that unites all Americans.

The Preamble

★ **The Preamble**
George Anastaplo

THE PREAMBLE TO THE CONSTITUTION STATES

We the People of the United States, in Order to form a more perfect Union, establish Justice, insure domestic Tranquility, provide for the common defence, promote the general Welfare, and secure the Blessings of Liberty to ourselves and our Posterity, do ordain and establish this CONSTITUTION for the United States of America.

It has long been assumed by some judges and commentators that the introduction to the Constitution of 1787—the Preamble—has no legal effect. Some have even dismissed it as adding little if anything to the Constitution. Such a belittling of the Preamble is not in keeping with how distinguished citizens at various times in United States history have regarded it. In 1819, for example, Chief Justice John Marshall, speaking for the Supreme Court in *McCulloch* v. *Maryland*, found support in the Preamble for the Court's decision that the national government should override state governments in matters about which the Constitution granted powers to Congress.

The actions of the South in 1861 give the most dramatic demonstration of the importance and the scope of the Preamble. When the leaders of the Confederacy began efforts to secede from the Union after Abraham Lincoln was elected president in 1860, they used the Preamble to the United States Constitution as the basis of the first draft of the constitution of the Confederate States of America.

This is the preamble to the constitution of the Confederacy written in 1861. Brackets show words that were taken out of the 1787 Preamble; italics show words that were added.

Confederacy the eleven Southern states that seceded from the United States of America 1860–1861

secede formally depart or withdraw from an organization

▶ The signing of the Constitution of the United States. George Washington is standing on a platform holding a copy of the document.

We the People of the [United] *Confederate* States, *each State acting in its sovereign and independent character*, in order to form a [more perfect Union] *permanent federal government*, establish Justice, insure domestic Tranquility, [provide for the common defence, promote the general Welfare,] and secure the Blessings of Liberty to ourselves and our Posterity—*invoking the favor and guidance of Almighty God*—do ordain and establish this Constitution for the [United] *Confederate* States of America.

The Confederate leaders added to their preamble a plea for "the favor and guidance of Almighty God." Perhaps they sensed that they would need divine favor in order to succeed in their effort to break up the Union. By replacing the phrase "a more perfect Union" with "a permanent federal government," the leaders emphasized the states' rights approach of the seceding states.

Another significant change was that the preamble of the Confederate constitution weakened the phrase "We the People" by adding that each state was "acting in its sovereign and independent character." Also important was that the provision "to promote the general Welfare" was removed. The phrase "to provide for the common defence" was removed from the preamble, but it was included in Article I, Section 8, of the Confederate constitution. Perhaps it was taken out because the word "common" suggested more a Union than a Confederation. These changes in the 1861 preamble show an expectation that the government under the new Confederate constitution would be much more dependent on the states than the national government had been under the Constitution of the United States.

The changes in the Confederate constitution of 1861 show how troublesome, even dangerous, the Constitution of 1787 and its preamble had seemed to the slaveholding states. The defeat of the Confederacy in the Civil War, with the abolition of slavery nationwide, reaffirmed and even strengthened the Constitution of the United States.

The Preamble to the Constitution of 1787 lists six objectives for which the nation's government was established. The first and last of these purposes—"to form a more perfect Union . . . and secure the Blessings of Liberty to ourselves and our Posterity"—were special to the new democratic order embodied by the Declaration of Independence in 1776. The other four objectives—to "establish Justice, insure domestic Tranquility, provide for the common defence, promote the general Welfare"—had long been expected of any serious national government. The Framers also understood that doubts and uncertainties in the body of the Constitution itself as well as other documents might be settled by considering the objectives in the Preamble.

Beginning the Constitution of 1787 with the phrase "We the People" has made the people of the United States more likely to regard themselves as one people—a people entitled to keep the country together and to have a national government powerful enough to carry out the objectives in the Preamble of the Constitution of the United States.

---

sovereign having complete independence in its relations with other nations or units of government

INTRODUCTION—Constitutional Concepts; Constitutional Origins

The preamble looks to the future. "We the people . . .," it reads, "do," not did, "ordain and establish this Constitution." Its authority depends upon the continuous consent of the governed. The document comes from its drafters but the law they create comes from the generation living under and enforcing it. "Posterity" is among the purposes the preamble lists for which it was created. Later constitutions around the world followed the idea of a preamble. The French Declaration of the Rights of Man and Citizen, drafted in 1789, became the preamble to the French Constitution of 1791.

Article I

All legislative powers granted herein shall be vested in a Congress of the United States, which shall consist of a Senate and a House of Representatives.

Congress
Morris S. Ogul

vest to grant with particular authority, property, and rights

Articles of Confederation the first constitution of the thirteen original United States; in effect 1781–1789

enumerated powers the powers listed in a constitution; these powers also are sometimes called the *expressed* powers

All constitutional regimes face the problem of what powers the government should have and what controls should be placed on it. The Framers of the Constitution dealt with these issues in terms of their experience with the Articles of Confederation. The Articles granted enumerated powers of government to the states. The Framers, however, shifted those powers to the national government, granting the enumerated powers to the Congress of the United States.

Limiting the authority of Congress by enumerating its powers was a bold move by the Framers. It was not fully effective, and it left many questions unanswered. What would happen, for example, if Congress had to deal with a problem that was not specifically covered in the enumerated powers listed in Article I? One answer was provided in the "necessary and proper clause" in Article I, Section 8. This provision allowed Congress broad choices about how it would act to carry out its expressed powers. A second answer was found in how the Constitution was interpreted over the years. Consequently, Article I, Section 1, enabled the Constitution to serve as a broad framework of government. It established Congress and the other two branches of government, which were able to adapt to changing political conditions and views as the nation itself developed.

President Eisenhower delivers his State of the Union address to a joint session of Congress on January 7, 1960.

Interpreting the Enumerated Powers

However, the answers to questions about the enumerated powers were incomplete. They depended on interpretations of the Constitution, and these interpretations would make its provisions mean what those interpreting it wanted it to mean. Through this process, the document could lose the meanings that the Framers intended. As a result, interpreting the Constitution proved both a virtue and a weakness. A flexible Constitution was necessary in a changing society, yet no one could be certain of its meaning until it was interpreted.

For example, does the power of Congress to "regulate commerce with foreign nations and among the several States" (Article I, Section 8) mean that Congress can prohibit child labor? For well over a century, the courts and Congress answered no. Then, in 1938, this interpretation changed after Congress and the courts agreed to ban child labor. In this way, although the Framers listed the exact powers of Congress in order to limit what Congress could do, their effort was only partly successful.

The Two Houses of Congress

bicameral having two chambers

Article I, Section 8, seeks to limit government and achieve a balance of power among the states. It tries to accomplish these goals by creating Congress as a bicameral national legislature. Representation in the House of Representatives is based on population. Each state has a specific number of seats in the House reflecting the size of its population. This gives an advantage to states with large numbers of citizens. In the Senate, however, each state has two senators, regardless of population. This provides an advantage to the states with small populations.

Providing for a bicameral legislature in Congress achieves an important political result by balancing the interests of the large and small states. At the same time, it helps achieve limited government. To become laws, all bills must pass the two houses of Congress. In this way, the Framers believed, all proposed laws would receive careful consideration. Laws might be harder to pass, but they would be more effective legislation. That, too, was intended to promote limited government.

The Power to Investigate

precedent established ruling, understanding, or practice of the law

The power of Congress to conduct investigations flows from its legislative powers. Although the Constitution does not mention congressional investigations, Congress and the courts have assumed that the Framers intended them to have this power. There also were important precedents for this interpretation. When the Constitution was written, state legislatures had the power to investigate. Moreover, the British parliament exercised this power as well.

Congress's power to investigate is considered necessary to provide its members with the information they need to create public policies. Congress also investigates the activities of the executive branch to ensure that executive departments and agencies are fully carrying out the specific provisions of the laws. Such investigations may also lead

Congress has a split personality and has had since the first Congress formed in 1789. It is a lawmaking institution that writes laws and makes policy for the whole country. It is also a representative assembly whose 535 elected officials must be responsive to constituents' demands. Members must balance national issues with local concerns. The Framers had these dual roles in mind when they designed a legislature elected from states and geographic districts.

In the last decades of the twentieth century, the constant pressure to raise money for campaigns has meant that legislators spend less time on congressional duties. Staff does much of the actual law drafting in committees that function much like little legislatures. This is where the main struggle over legislation takes place. Congress itself resembles a collection of committees.

see also

INTRODUCTION—Constitutional Concepts; Constitutional Origins

Congress to consider restructuring or reforming executive agencies that may be at fault.

Congress and the Executive Branch

Can Congress delegate its legislative power to the other branches of government? Although some decisions by the Supreme Court suggest that Congress cannot, most of the evidence in fact shows that Congress delegates its powers regularly. It follows this practice particularly when standards are included in the legislation it passes for carrying out such delegation. The executive branch, then, often is expected to fill in the details that Congress does not cover. For example, Congress allows the licensing of broadcast stations by the executive branch if this licensing promotes the public interest, convenience, or necessity. Such a vague standard thus puts the executive agencies responsible for regulating broadcasting in charge of granting these licenses. Congress also delegates power on a contingency basis. That means an executive department or agency can determine that certain conditions require it to use such power.

Foreign affairs provides the clearest example of the executive branch's exercise of legislative power. Here, such delegation of power is necessary because swift action is required, and Congress cannot act decisively and quickly. Moreover, the president's power as commander in chief is granted but not precisely defined in the Constitution. Thus, in foreign affairs, the line between legislative powers and executive powers can become blurred.

Article I, Section 1, establishes the principle that government actions must be based on the basic law of the Constitution. However, this provision does not offer complete and final answers about what public policies are permissible. Nor does it establish clear boundary lines between legislative and executive powers. The nation's political experience addresses those problems, but they have never been solved. Nor will they ever be. Public policies have changed over time and will continue to do so as the United States plays new roles in world affairs. Nevertheless, this section of the Constitution highlights the enduring value of peaceful, orderly resolution of governmental disputes under the fundamental law.

House of Representatives
Robert F. Drinan, S.J.

vest to grant with particular authority, property, and rights

ARTICLE I, SECTIONS 1 AND 2, OF THE CONSTITUTION STATE

*Section 1. All legislative Powers herein granted shall be **vested** in a Congress of the United States, which shall consist of a Senate and House of Representatives.*

Section 2. The House shall be composed of Members chosen every second Year by the People of the several States, and the Electors in each State shall have the qualifications requisite for Electors of the most numerous Branch of the State Legislature.

No Person shall be Representative who shall not have attained to the Age of twenty-five Years, and been seven Years a Citizen of the United States, and who shall not, when elected, be an Inhabitant of that State in which he shall be chosen.

apportion divide proportionally or share according to a plan, such as representatives or taxes under a government

*Representatives and direct Taxes shall be **apportioned** among the several States which may be included within this Union, according to their respective Numbers, which shall be determined by adding to the whole number of free Persons, including those bound to Service for a Term of Years, and excluding Indians not taxed, three fifths of all other Persons. The actual Enumeration shall be made within three Years after the first Meeting of the Congress of the United States, and within every subsequent Term of ten Years, in such Manner as they shall by Law direct. The number of Representatives shall not exceed one for every thirty Thousand, but each State shall have at Least one Representative; and until such enumeration shall be made, the State of New Hampshire shall be entitled to chuse three, Massachusetts eight, Rhode-Island and Providence Plantations one, Connecticut five, New York six, New Jersey four, Pennsylvania eight, Delaware one, Maryland six, Virginia ten, North Carolina five, South Carolina five, and Georgia three.*

When vacancies happen in the Representation from any State, the Executive Authority thereof shall issue Writs of Election to fill such Vacancies.

*The House of Representatives shall chuse their Speaker and other Officers; and shall have the sole power of **Impeachment**.*

impeachment method by which the House of Representatives may charge the nation's highest-ranking officials, including the president, with wrongdoing; following impeachment, if the officials are found guilty of the charges, the Senate then may try them and remove them from office

The government of the United States is divided into three branches: the executive, the legislative, and the judicial. The legislative branch, or Congress, is the branch of government responsible for making the laws. Congress is divided into two separate bodies, the Senate and the House of Representatives. The Framers of the Constitution had strong disagreements about how the legislative branch of government should be organized. These disagreements were resolved at the Constitutional Convention by what became known as the Great Compromise—a national legislature made up of two houses.

The Great Compromise

The Framers' debate in 1787 over the legislative branch was fueled by the American colonists' bitter experiences when they lacked meaningful representation in the British government. Because the Framers regarded representation in political affairs to be of key importance, the question of how the legislative branch should be organized became a central issue at the Constitutional Convention. Two main proposals were considered.

bicameral having two chambers

The Virginia Plan, supported by the large states, proposed a bicameral legislature, in which a state's representation would be based on its wealth or population. The New Jersey Plan, supported by the smaller states, proposed a legislature in which each state would have the same number of representatives, without regard to its population or wealth.

The Framers finally agreed to the Great Compromise, which created a bicameral legislature called Congress. The House of Representatives reflects the interests of the large states as embodied in the Virginia Plan, since each state's number of representatives is based on its population. The Senate, in contrast, reflects the interest of the smaller states as embodied in the New Jersey Plan, since each state has two senators regardless of its population.

Qualifications of Members

Article I, Section 2, of the Constitution establishes the structure of the House of Representatives. Members of the House are chosen every second year and serve two-year terms. Such frequent elections give the people more control over the actions of representatives. This two-year term is balanced in theory by the six-year terms of the members of the Senate. Section 2 also requires that representatives must be at least twenty-five years old, citizens of the United States for at least seven years, and citizens of the states they represent. By custom, House members live in the districts they represent.

The Issue of Term Limits

As of the end of the twentieth century, there was no constitutional limit to the number of terms that members of the House may serve, but limiting the number of terms for House members had become an important political issue in the 1990s. Those who favored term limits argued that representatives must spend so much time running and raising funds for reelection that they might be too willing to go along with the political interests of the majority. Supporters insisted that term limits would ensure that the membership of the House would regularly change, and this steady turnover would foster new ideas and help speed up its slow-moving, bureaucratic pace.

Those who opposed term limits argued that the responsiveness of the House to the people's will is its great strength. They believed that representatives who have served for a number of terms bring valuable experience to the institution. Most important, they pointed out that term limits would keep many well-qualified, popular representatives from being elected again, even though the voters in their districts may have wanted them to remain in office.

In 1995, the Supreme Court ruled in a 5-to-4 decision that no state may limit the number of terms to which its voters may elect members of congress. This decision indicates that an amendment to the Constitution may be required in order to limit congressional terms.

The size of the House of Representatives makes it unwieldy. To make it function efficiently, the House needs both good organization and effective leadership. A strong Speaker of the House can exert great influence. He is the presiding officer and traditionally the leader of the majority party. Some speakers become national figures, such as Thomas P. (Tip) O'Neill, a Boston Democrat, in the 1980s and Newt Gingrich, a Georgia Republican, in the 1990s.

Any member of the House can introduce legislation. This is usually called a bill. The Speaker refers the bills to appropriate committees. Sometimes the committees hold hearings on the bills in order to prepare them for consideration by the full House. The Committee on Rules regulates debate on the House floor. It recommends the length of time to be devoted to each bill and the conditions under which amendments may be considered. The full House approves the Committee on Rules' recommendations before the full House debates the bill. After debate and any amendments, the House votes, usually electronically.

Membership of the House

The number of seats in the House held by each state is determined by the census every ten years. Article I, Section 2, of the Constitution sets forth the original apportionment plan. However, as the country grew, this provision became outdated. If it had been continued, the House would now have more than several thousand members. Therefore, in 1929 Congress limited the size of the House of Representatives to 435 voting members, with each member, on average, representing about 500,000 **constituents**. When a House seat becomes vacant due to death, resignation, or other circumstances, the governor of the state calls a special election to fill the vacancy.

The Speaker of the House leads the House of Representatives. Article I, Section 2, provides for the election of the Speaker and other officers of the House. The Speaker is selected by the caucus of the majority party, and then is formally elected by the entire House membership. The Speaker is not required to be a member of the House, but the practice has been to elect the leader of the majority party. The Speaker is second in the line of presidential succession, after the Vice President.

The Powers of Congress

The powers of the legislative branch, like those of the other branches of government, are limited only to those that are **enumerated** in the Constitution. The Framers were determined to limit the power of government only as much as necessary. Therefore, the Constitution grants relatively few powers exclusively to Congress. One of these is the power to impeach officials of the United States. It is important to note that to impeach does not mean to force an official to resign. If the full House votes to impeach, the Senate then must try the official. He or she may be removed from office if two-thirds of the Senate vote to convict.

The House of Representatives has impeached only one president—Andrew Johnson, in 1868. However, the Senate did not convict him, falling one vote short of the required two-thirds majority. The House almost impeached President Richard Nixon in 1974 as a result of the Watergate scandal. The House Committee on the Judiciary began impeachment proceedings and recommended impeachment on three counts. The House ended its action when President Nixon resigned, shortly after the Supreme Court ordered him to release the incriminating Watergate tapes.

Perhaps the most important power of the House of Representatives is the power of the purse—taxing and spending. The Constitution requires that all revenue bills must originate in the House. One of the features of British rule most detested by the American colonists was "taxation without representation." Therefore, the Framers made sure that taxation would be kept in check by requiring that all tax measures be introduced in the House, since that body was most responsive to the will of the people. In practice the Senate can influence or even propose revenue measures through the process of amending bills that are before it.

constituent a voter in a district who elects an official for representation

enumerated powers the powers listed in a constitution; these powers also are sometimes called the *expressed* powers

 see also

▶ Legislators pack the House chamber at the Capitol to hear President Reagan give his 1983 State of the Union Address.

★ **United States Senate**
Sarah A. Binder

president *pro tempore* (Latin, "for the time being") serving as president on a temporary basis

ARTICLE I, SECTION 3, OF THE CONSTITUTION STATES

The Senate of the United States shall be composed of two Senators from each State, chosen by the Legislatures thereof, for six Years; and each Senator shall have one Vote.

Immediately after they shall be assembled in Consequence of the first Election, they shall be divided as equally as may be into three Classes. The Seats of the Senators of the first Class shall be vacated at the Expiration of the second Year, of the second Class at the Expiration of the fourth Year, and of the third Class at the Expiration of the sixth Year, so that one-third may be chosen every second Year; and if Vacancies happen by Resignation, or otherwise, during the Recess of the Legislature of any State, the Executive thereof may make temporary Appointments until the next Meeting of the Legislature, which shall then fill such Vacancies.

No Person shall be a Senator who shall not have attained to the Age of thirty Years, and been nine Years a Citizen of the United States, and who shall not, when elected, be an inhabitant of that State for which he shall be chosen.

The Vice President of the United States shall be President of the Senate, but shall have no vote, unless they be equally divided.

*The Senate shall chuse their other Officers, and also a **President pro tempore**, in the absence of the Vice President, or when he shall exercise the Office of President of the United States.*

impeachment method by which the House of Representatives may charge the nation's highest-ranking officials, including the president, with wrongdoing; following impeachment, if the officials are found guilty of the charges, the Senate then may try them and remove them from office

*The Senate shall have the sole Power to try all **Impeachments**. When sitting for that purpose they shall be on Oath or Affirmation. When the President of the United States is tried, the Chief Justice shall preside: And no person shall be convicted without the Concurrence of two thirds of the Members present.*

Judgment in Cases of Impeachment shall not extend further than to removal from Office, and disqualification to hold and enjoy any Office of honor, Trust, or Profit under the United States; but the Party convicted shall nevertheless be liable and subject to Indictment, Trial, Judgment, and Punishment, according to Law.

The Senate is established in Article I, Section 3, of the Constitution as the upper chamber of the United States Congress. A number of important provisions in Section 3 distinguish the Senate from the House of Representatives, making them very different legislative bodies.

The provisions for the Senate were the result of political compromise by the delegates to the Constitutional Convention in 1787. The delegates from the large states insisted that representation in Congress be based on population, giving these states more votes than states with small populations. The delegates from the small states insisted just as strongly on equal representation of both large and small states, to prevent the large states from harming the interests of the small states.

The solution reached by the Framers is called the Connecticut Compromise, or sometimes the Great Compromise. Without it, the Convention might well have broken up. A bicameral legislature was created. In the House of Representatives, the lower chamber, representation is based on state population. So the large states have more seats than the small states. In the Senate, the upper chamber, each state has two seats so that representation is the same for all states regardless of population. Because each senator is entitled to one vote, small and large states have equal power in the Senate. As a result of the Connecticut Compromise, Article I, Section 7, of the Constitution also provides that the House of Representatives has sole power to originate bills to raise and spend money. The Senate has the power only to amend or reject the revenue bills from the House.

bicameral having two chambers

Features of the Senate

In the provisions of Article I, Section 3, the Framers sought to protect the Senate from pressures and demands by the public. First, members of the Senate were to be chosen by state legislatures, not directly elected by the public as House members were. Second, senators were to serve six-year terms rather than two-year terms as House members did. Third, senators were divided into three groups, so that only one-third of the Senate would be elected every two years. These longer, staggered terms meant that the members of the Senate would be chosen at different times and by different groups of state legislators. Fourth, state governors were

The United States Senate.

The Senate prides itself on its traditions. Courtesy is high among senators, who are rarely personal toward each other. The Senate is informal for a legislative body and prides itself on allowing unlimited debate. A senator speaking on the Senate floor does not have to stop. Southern senators long used the **filibuster** to tie up the Senate in order to keep civil rights issues from coming to a vote. In 1957 South Carolina Senator Strom Thurmond spoke continuously against a proposed civil rights bill for a record 24 hours and 18 minutes. The Senate also likes to call itself "the world's greatest deliberative body." Matters are considered so much that one nineteenth-century senator, Henry Wilson, said, "I believe if we introduced the Lord's Prayer here, senators would propose a large number of amendments to it."

filibuster prolonged floor debate aimed at defeating measures by preventing a final vote

given the power to make temporary appointments to fill vacant Senate seats, unlike the House, where special elections were held to fill vacant seats. Fifth, senators were required to be at least thirty years old, in contrast to representatives, who were required to be only twenty-five years old; and senators were required to be citizens at least nine years, two years longer than required for House members. Together, the Framers intended that these provisions would make the Senate a wiser, more elite, and more stable legislative body than the House. They also believed such provisions made it more likely that the Senate would serve as a check against the people as well as against the House.

Article I, Section 3, also contains an important provision regarding the leadership of the Senate. It provides that the vice president of the United States serve as president of the Senate and preside over sessions of the Senate. The vice president also has the power to cast a vote in case of a tie, when the Senate is evenly divided. If the vice president is absent, the Senate chooses a president *pro tempore*. Modern vice presidents have rarely exercised their power to preside over the Senate, except when it appeared that their vote might be needed to break a tie on an important issue.

Senators have been very reluctant to give the presiding officer any power under the rules to lead the Senate. Rivalries between the legislative and executives branches, as well as between the two political parties, have made senators wary of giving too much power to the Senate president. Senators consider what might happen when the vice president is a member of the opposite political party or disagrees with the priorities of the Senate.

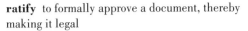

ratify to formally approve a document, thereby making it legal

Popular Election of Senators

One of the key provisions of Article I, Section 3, was revised when the Seventeenth Amendment was **ratified** in 1913. That amendment changed the method of selecting senators. It requires the states to select senators through direct election by the people. By the end of the nineteenth century, many states already had changed to a form of direct election, even though the Constitution itself was not amended for this purpose until 1913. Reformers aimed at making the Senate a more democratic body by ending the practice of state legislatures appointing senators. Yet even after the adoption of the Seventeenth Amendment, the Senate has remained more protected from public pressures than the House. Because senators still serve staggered six-year terms, the Senate is less likely to be swayed by temporary popular trends.

Debate in the Senate

The Senate is usually thought of as a chamber with unlimited debate, where any member can stand on the Senate floor and filibuster any bill or amendment he or she disagrees with. While this picture of the Senate is largely true, it has resulted from custom and practice rather than constitutional requirements. Surprisingly, the Constitution says very little about how the Senate should conduct its legislative business. For example, Article I, Section 3, makes no provision about how long senators can debate a bill, and Article I, Section 5, gives the Senate (as well as the House) the power to make its own rules of procedure. Although the Framers intended the Senate to be the smaller, more deliberative chamber, they left the decisions about the rules of Senate debate to the senators themselves.

Special Powers of the Senate

The Framers granted special powers to the Senate in only a few areas. In each case, their intent was to share power between the House and Senate or between the Senate and the president so that each could check and restrain the other's powers. First, the power to impeach officials of the executive and legislative branches is divided between the House and Senate. Article I, Section 2, grants the House the power to impeach an official, but only the Senate can "try" him or her and vote to convict. Most important, a two-thirds vote of the Senate is required for impeachment.

Second, under Article II, Section 2, the president is required to seek the advice and consent of the Senate for high-ranking appointments, such as cabinet officers, ambassadors, federal judges, and Supreme Court justices, and in making treaties with other nations. In both cases, a two-thirds concurring vote of the Senate is required. The Senate's role in confirming appointments and in ratifying treaties ensures that the conduct of the nation's domestic and foreign policy is shared by the executive and legislative branches of government.

INTRODUCTION—Constitutional Origins; ARTICLE I—House of Representatives; The Impeachment Power; Members of Congress; Organization of Congress; The Unwritten Constitution in Congress; ARTICLE II—The Appointments Power; SEVENTEENTH AMENDMENT

The Impeachment Power
Michael J. Gerhardt

indictment a formal written statement charging a person or persons with an offense after a grand jury has examined the evidence and found that there is a valid case

ratify to formally approve a document, thereby making it legal

ARTICLE I, SECTION 2, CLAUSE 5, OF THE CONSTITUTION STATES

The House of Representatives shall chuse their Speaker and other Officers; and shall have the sole Power of Impeachment.

ARTICLE I, SECTION 3, CLAUSES 6 & 7, OF THE CONSTITUTION STATES

The Senate shall have the sole Power to try all Impeachments. When sitting for that purpose they shall be on Oath or Affirmation. When the President of the United States is tried, the Chief Justice shall preside: And no person shall be convicted without the Concurrence of two thirds of the Members present.

Judgments in cases of Impeachment shall not extend further than to removal from Office, and disqualification to hold and enjoy any Office of honor, Trust, or Profit under the United States: but the Party convicted shall nevertheless be liable and subject to Indictment, Judgment, and Punishment, according to Law.

The power of impeachment enables Congress to confront leaders of the other two branches of government who may be guilty of serious misconduct. The House has the power to bring charges of wrongdoing, and the Senate has the power to hold a trial to decide whether these charges are true.

The Framers of the Constitution intended impeachment to be a powerful weapon—but a difficult one to use. Yet some of the Framers and the delegates to the state conventions that ratified the Constitution worried that granting Congress the impeachment power made Congress superior to the president. But the impeachment process has not worked out as its early supporters or critics envisioned. From the adoption of the Constitution through the late 1990s, the House has formally impeached only fifteen officials.

The Senate tried and convicted seven of these, acquitted five more, dismissed two, and did not proceed against one official who resigned before his removal trial began. In addition, several other federal officials, including President Richard Nixon in 1974, resigned from office after the House started, but before it completed, impeachment hearings.

In *The Federalist*, No. 65, dated March 7, 1788, Alexander Hamilton defined impeachment in the following terms:

"[Impeachment is a] method of national inquest into the conduct of public men."

Party Politics and Impeachment

Loyalty to political parties has been less of a driving force in the impeachment process than some Framers feared. In the nineteenth century, heated partisan differences over the proper use of power in the federal government led to six impeachments, including those of Justice Samuel Chase of the Supreme Court in 1804, and of President Andrew Johnson in 1868. Both trials were marked by intense debate about the need to avoid the dangers partisan impeachments pose to the security of future presidents and Supreme Court justices. Yet no conviction was ever based on strictly partisan grounds or decided by a party-driven vote. In fact, the

The opening of the high court of impeachment for President Johnson in 1868.

cases of Chase and Johnson served to discourage later impeachments motivated by personal or political unpopularity.

The Douglas and Nixon Impeachment Attempts

Party politics played no part in the outcomes of the two major post-World War II impeachment attempts—against Justice William O. Douglas in 1970 and President Richard M. Nixon in 1974.

In Justice Douglas's case, a few Republican members in the House deeply disliked his rulings on the Court and his lifestyle, which included four marriages. These political differences led to the impeachment inquiry against him. But the House took no formal action after it investigated the charges against him and found no basis for questioning his performance in office.

The case of President Nixon, a Republican, was a result of the Watergate scandal. Before the 1972 presidential elections, Republican Party spies broke into the national headquarters of the Democratic Party at the Watergate office building in Washington, D.C. As the details became known, President Nixon was accused of involvement in the operation, perhaps even directing it. He was also charged with obstructing the criminal investigation into the break-in. In the early stages of the investigation, Nixon's fellow Republicans in Congress strongly supported him against the charges of an impeachable offense. Then, in early August of 1974, the House Judiciary Committee approved three articles of impeachment that charged President Nixon with obstruction of justice, abuse of powers, and unlawful refusal to supply material subpoenaed by the House. All of the Republicans on the committee opposed all three articles.

subpoena a court order requiring a person to appear to present testimony or documents

Behind the scenes, key Republicans encouraged the president to resign, because they believed that he was likely to be impeached and removed from office. After President Nixon released tapes of conversations that proved his involvement in the Watergate break-in, he lost nearly all his support among Republicans in Congress. The willingness by most Republicans to go beyond party politics regarding Nixon's impeachment and their urging him to resign made his leaving office unavoidable.

▶ Ticket issued for President Andrew Johnson's impeachment trial.

> Richard Nixon has acted in a manner contrary to his trust as President and subversive of constitutional government, to the great prejudice of law and justice and to the manifest injury of the people of the United States.
>
> —U.S. House of Representatives, Judiciary Committee, *Articles of Impeachment,* July 27, 1974

Nineteenth- Versus Twentieth-Century Practices

Other changes in the impeachment process in the twentieth century threw doubt on its fairness. Members of Congress, particularly senators, had not been spending much time or taking much interest in impeachment matters. Legislators' involvement was different than in the nineteenth century, when the full Senate sat through the entire impeachment trials. Only a handful of senators attended the trials of Judge Harold Louderback in 1932 and Judge Halsted Ritter in 1937. In fact, Senate attendance was so poor for Judge Ritter's trial that the lawmakers drafted a rule allowing the Senate to appoint a special committee to do all the fact-finding for such removal trials. In the 1980s, the Senate used such committees in the removal trials of three federal district court judges. Many senators who voted to remove the judges admitted that they were not familiar with the records compiled by the trial committees.

The reasons for the Senate's changed attitude toward impeachment are easy to understand. Congress is expected to pass laws in many more areas than ever in the past. Members of Congress have been spending much more time preparing for their reelection, and few of them regard the impeachment of lower court judges as important to that goal. Both houses of Congress appointed special committees to oversee the executive branch's enforcement of the laws. These oversight committees helped investigate, embarrass, and pressure impeachable officials and publicize their possible misconduct. By making officials accountable for their conduct in office, these committees have often made recourse to impeachment unnecessary.

In the late 1980s, a federal district court judge, Walter Nixon, was impeached, convicted, and removed from office. He then challenged the constitutionality of the Senate oversight committee. The Constitution, he claimed, granted "the sole power to try impeachments" to the Senate and required the full Senate to take part in every step of a removal trial. The Supreme Court rejected Judge Nixon's challenge on the ground that Congress had the power to decide how to carry out impeachment procedures and trials.

high crimes and misdemeanors any or all of the following types of conduct: (1) a serious offense against the federal government, (2) criminal misconduct for which an official can be indicted, tried, and convicted, or (3) misconduct that violates a criminal law, constitutes a serious offense against the federal government, and relates to the performance of his or her official duties

nonindictable not subject to being charged with a crime by a grand jury

perjury the willful breaking of an oath either by telling a lie or omitting to do what has been promised under the oath

---

Justice Samuel Chase angered Republicans by constantly and publicly attacking their politics and leaders. He also helped in the convictions of several prominent Republicans for **sedition** and **treason**. His rulings against two such Republicans became the main reason that the Republican-controlled Congress tried to impeach and remove him from office in 1804. After the House impeached Chase, the Senate acquitted him, even though twenty-five of the thirty-six members were Republicans.

In 1868, the Republican-controlled House impeached President Andrew Johnson, a Democrat, on the grounds that he had illegally removed a cabinet officer and that he had failed to enforce Reconstruction and other legislation. The Senate failed to convict him by one vote.

---

sedition incitement of resistance to or insurrection against lawful authority

treason the offense of attempting to overthrow the government

Organization of Congress
Norman Ornstein

High Crimes and Misdemeanors

The kinds of misconduct for which officials may be impeached have also changed over time. The Framers generally agreed that **high crimes and misdemeanors** included serious offenses against the national government or other violations of criminal law. Yet most of the fifteen officials impeached were tried and removed on the basis of **nonindictable** offenses. Nevertheless, the Senate has tended to convict officials impeached by the House on the basis of crimes for which they could have been indicted, tried, and convicted. In the 1980s the Senate convicted and removed from office three federal district judges for tax fraud, bribery, and **perjury**—all indictable offenses.

Should Judges Be Impeached for Doing Their Job?

In the 1990s, Congress debated whether federal judges may be impeached and removed from office because of their court rulings. In 1996, some Republican members of the House introduced impeachment resolutions against three federal district judges who, they charged, had deliberately misinterpreted the Constitution. Those who supported their impeachment argued that these judges' decisions were in conflict with the Constitution, thus necessarily illegal, and nonindictable offenses for which the judges could be impeached.

Those opposing the impeachments countered that the value of the federal judiciary depends on its insulation from political retaliation for unpopular decisions. Federal judges, they argued, have a basic duty to protect individual rights and minority rights against hostile majorities.

The final judgment about whether and how to exercise the impeachment power rests with Congress. Many commentators and members of Congress fear that Congress's failure to exercise the impeachment power more aggressively may lead to unfair proceedings or allow corrupt government officials to escape punishment. Whether these concerns are founded or not, what is clear is that Congress's approach to impeachment is unlikely to change until there is pressure on it to do so. Impeachment probably will remain Congress's special "one-hundred-ton gun"—a weapon awesome to behold but almost impossible to use effectively.

ARTICLE I, SECTION 4, OF THE CONSTITUTION STATES

The Times, Places, and Manner of holding Elections for Senators and Representatives, shall be prescribed in each State by the Legislature thereof; but the Congress may at any time by Law make or alter such Regulations, except as to the Places chusing Senators.

The Congress shall assemble at least once in every Year, and such Meeting shall be on the first Monday in December, unless they shall by Law appoint a different Day.

The Constitution originally decreed that Congress would meet in the first week of December each year. But that same clause allowed Congress to pass a law to change this date if it chose. As things turned out, Congress decided it needed to do so. Both Congress and the president are elected in November, but the Constitution provided for the president to be sworn into office the following March. To make it easier for the legislative and executive branches to work together, the Twentieth Amendment was added in 1933. It changed the date the president takes office to January 20 following the presidential election, and moved the date Congress meets to January 3 after the congressional election. As a result, each new Congress, elected in early November of every even-numbered year, consists of two year-long sessions that start on January 3 of the following odd-numbered year.

Running Congress

When the new Congress convenes, its first order of business is to choose its leaders and set its rules. For the House of Representatives, that means selecting a Speaker and for the Senate, a majority leader.

Since all the members of the House are up for election every two years, the House rules are not considered as ongoing, and they are voted on as a package at the beginning of each new Congress. But since only one-third of the members of the Senate are up for election every two years, it is a continuing body, and its rules are ongoing, even though senators vote on them at the start of the new Congress to reflect any changes.

The Constitution explicitly gives Congress full oversight of its own affairs. Each house determines its own rules and procedures within certain guidelines laid down in the Constitution. The Constitution requires each house to keep a journal of its proceedings as a public record; it also requires a two-thirds vote to expel a member. From the beginning of the Republic, the rules and traditions of Congress have been very important in setting the tone of its debates and the policies of the nation.

Committees of Congress

In many ways, the House and the Senate have similar structures and organizations. The committee system is perhaps the most important working tool they have in common, with most of the committees in both houses very close in name and jurisdiction. The committees are made up of a fairly small number of members, and in both houses committee names and areas of authority are usually similar. The first Congress, which met in 1789, had no permanent committees, but created a committee when each bill was introduced. But it soon became clear that Congress needed a more efficient way to work, and within a few years both houses set up a number of permanent committees. Those committees have authority over and responsibility for specific subjects, such as the budget, veterans' affairs, and foreign policy. The permanent committees usually divide their work even further, creating subcommittees to handle different aspects of legislation.

> "Congress in session is Congress on public exhibition, whilst Congress in its Committee rooms is Congress at work."
>
> —Woodrow Wilson (1854–1924), twenty-eighth president of the United States

jurisdiction the territory or area within which authority may be exercised

Lyndon Johnson, before he was vice president and president in the 1960s, was likely the most successful Senate majority leader in American history. He held that position from 1954 through 1960. One Senate colleague, J. William Fulbright, said that Johnson was "a master at managing the Senate and at reconciling people with diametrically opposed views. Nobody could match him. He knew every personal interest of every member of the Senate just like he knew the palm of his hand. He knew how to bring people together because he could appeal to their different interests."

ratify to formally approve a document, thereby making it legal

president *pro tempore* (Latin, "for the time being") serving as president on a temporary basis

Both the House and the Senate select committee members from the majority and minority political parties. The chair of each committee is a member of the majority party. Generally, the chair is the most senior member of the committee—that is, the member who has served on the committee the longest.

Powerful Committees

The most important committees in each house have similar but not identical areas of authority and responsibilities. The money committees—those that have taxing and spending power—are very important: they include each house's Appropriations Committee, the House Ways and Means Committee, and the Senate Finance Committee. The Senate Foreign Relations Committee, too, has always had great influence, because the Senate has unique powers in foreign affairs. These include the power to ratify all treaties and to approve all top officials nominated by the president, such as ambassadors and the secretaries of state and of defense.

The House of Representatives has one powerful committee without a strong Senate parallel—the Rules Committee. The Senate, with only 100 members, allows more open and free debate. That is not possible in the House, with 435 members. If each member were to speak for only two minutes each day, that debate would last fourteen and a half hours! So the House regulates debate and amendments on its bills. The House Rules Committee, like a traffic cop, sets the amount of time debate can last and what can be discussed, as well as the type of amendments members can add to a bill. This authority gives the Rules Committee an impact on the final shape of the bill itself.

Just as Congressional committees are organized along party lines, so is Congress itself. Although there is an occasional member of a third political party or an independent, nearly all members of Congress are either Democrats or Republicans. Congress's leadership reflects the party-based organization as well.

Leadership in Congress

The leader of the House of Representatives is called the Speaker of the House. According to the Constitution, this officer is to be chosen by all the members of the House. In practice, the Speaker is chosen in a secret ballot by the members of the majority party who then vote for that person in an open session of the whole House. The Speaker of the House is both its most powerful leader and the leader of the majority party.

In the Senate, by contrast, the vice president presides, but this official lacks the powers of the Speaker of the House. The vice president's only real power in the Senate is that, as presiding officer, he or she can break tie votes on bills presented there. The Senate also elects a president *pro tempore* whose role is to preside in the vice president's absence. This is largely an honorary role that by tradition is given to the most senior member of the Senate. But the Senate's real counterpart to the House Speaker is the majority leader, who is chosen by the majority party.

Committees in both houses are powerful but some are more prestigious than others. Here, CIA Deputy Director Vernon A. Walters testifies before the Senate Watergate committee, 1974.

see also

ARTICLE I—House of Representatives; Members of Congress; United States Senate; The Unwritten Constitution in Congress; TWENTIETH AMENDMENT

whip a member of the House appointed to enforce party discipline and members' attendance at important sessions

caucus a meeting of persons of the same political party to select candidates or to decide on policy

sergeant-at-arms an officer of Congress who preserves order and executes commands

In addition to their top leaders, each house has its own leadership structure. In the House, the majority party elects a majority leader to help run the floor operations, including scheduling debates and votes on bills. The party also elects a majority whip to gather support from its members for bills the party favors and to ensure that members are present when important votes take place. The majority party also selects the head of its caucus, who presides over meetings of its members, where they select members of congressional committees and do research on legislation. In the same way, the minority political party in the House selects a minority leader, a minority whip, and other leaders as well. The Senate has a similar structure in the leadership of its majority and minority parties.

In both houses, the majority party selects the officers, such as the clerk of the House, the secretary of the Senate, and the two sergeants-at-arms, who help run Congress and the Capitol building itself, which, at the close of the twentieth century, were large complexes of more than 30,000 workers.

★ Procedural Rules of Congress
Walter E. Volkomer

quorum the number of members required to be present for a vote to take place

ARTICLE I, SECTION 5, OF THE CONSTITUTION STATES

Clause 1. *Each House shall be the Judge of the Elections, Returns, and Qualifications of its own Members, and a Majority of each shall constitute a **Quorum** to do Business; but a small Number may adjourn from day to day, and may be authorized to compel the Attendance of absent Members, in such Manner, and under such Penalties as each House may provide.*

Clause 2. *Each House may determine the Rules of its Proceedings, punish its Members for disorderly Behavior, and, with the Concurrence of two thirds, expel a Member.*

Clause 3. *Each House shall keep a Journal of its Proceedings, and from time to time publish the same, excepting such Parts as may in their Judgment require Secrecy; and the Yeas and Nays of the Members of either House on any question shall, at the Desire of one fifth of those Present, be entered in the Journal.*

Clause 4. Neither House, during the Session of Congress, shall, without the Consent of the other, adjourn for more than three days, nor to any other Place than that in which the two Houses shall be sitting.

Clause 1: Judging Elections

Clause 1 of Section 5 gives each house the power to judge both general and primary elections to Congress. On those occasions when Congress uses this authority, it acts in a judicial, not a legislative, capacity. The Senate and the House of Representatives do not share their power over these elections with any other branch of government. Nor do state or federal courts have any authority to act in this area. Congress also has the authority to conduct investigations and to require the testimony of witnesses and the production of evidence. When congressional elections are disputed in the Senate or the House, that body usually refers the issue to a committee. The committee then conducts an investigation and reports its findings to the full chamber.

Clause 2: Refusing to Seat Members

Clause 2 of Section 5 defines the powers of Congress over its members. For much of American history, Congress took the position that it had broad power to prevent elected members from taking their seats. Specifically, Congress asserted that its power here was not limited to excluding persons who did not meet the constitutional requirements of age,

House Speaker John W. McCormack (left) and Representative Adam Clayton Powell part company after the House voted to refuse to seat Powell in the Ninetieth Congress (1967).

sedition incitement of resistance to or insurrection against lawful authority

citizenship, and state residence found in Article I, Sections 2 and 3. On three occasions in the twentieth century, the House of Representatives voted to exclude elected members who met these constitutional requirements. In 1919 and again in 1920, a Wisconsin socialist legislator was denied his seat because he had been convicted of **sedition** during World War I. In a widely publicized 1967 case, the House voted to exclude New York's representative, Adam Clayton Powell.

Congressman Powell had served many terms in the House, representing Harlem, the largely African-American district in New York City. At the start of the 90th Congress in 1967, he was barred from taking his seat because of a number of serious legal and ethical problems he faced both in Congress and in the New York State courts. Powell then claimed that he had been denied his seat illegally. He sued to regain it, as well as his back salary.

In the case of *Powell* v. *McCormack* (1969), the Supreme Court defined the scope of Congress's power to exclude members. It upheld Powell's claim and ruled that Congress could not refuse to seat an elected legislator except on the basis of the three requirements for membership given in Article I, Sections 2 and 3, of the Constitution. First, representatives in the House must be at least twenty-five years of age and citizens of the United States for at least seven years when they are elected. Similarly, senators must be at least thirty years old and citizens for at least nine years. Second, both representatives and senators must also be residents of the state they are to represent at the time of the election. Third, Article I, Section 6, Clause 2, of the Constitution declares that no member of Congress can hold any other "office under the United States." A newly elected legislator must resign from any other judicial or executive position before taking office.

Clause 2: Disciplining Members of Congress

The Constitution is clear about the broad power of each house of Congress to discipline members who misbehave. The punishments that each house has used range from mild to severe. They include fines, loss of a committee-chair position, reprimand, and formal censure. Each of these penalties requires only a formal majority vote by the House or Senate.

Confederacy the eleven Southern states that seceded from the United States of America 1860–1861

The harshest punishment is expulsion. The Constitution specifically grants each house this power but requires that each proceeding be approved by a two-thirds vote. This penalty has been used in both houses. Fifteen senators have been expelled. One senator was expelled in 1797. The other fourteen were dismissed during the Civil War, because they supported the **Confederacy**. Nine more expulsion proceedings have occurred since then, but they were not successful. Only four members of the House have been expelled. Three of them were ousted during the Civil War, and the fourth expelled in 1980. The latter had been convicted of corruption; he was later reelected to office by the voters of his district. In some other cases, members have resigned rather than face expulsion proceedings.

Clause 2: Rules of Procedure

All organizations must have rules of procedure. In the case of Congress, the Constitution grants each house the authority to create its own rules of conduct. The House of Representatives has many complex rules; the Senate has fewer and less difficult rules. Much of the difference can be explained by the larger size of the House; thus the House must have more rules to ensure that it operates in an orderly manner. In the House, the time for debate by members is limited. On the other hand, the Senate operates on the basis of the unanimous consent of all members. The right to engage in the unlimited filibuster is a significant part of Senate tradition. Debate can be limited only by the use of Senate Rule 22. That rule provides that debate can be limited when three fifths of the entire Senate, or sixty members, vote for cloture.

In each house, changes in the rules of procedure can be made by simple majority vote. For example, in 1995 the Republican-controlled House of Representatives voted to require a three-fifths majority to pass all bills to increase taxes.

Clause 3: A Record of Proceedings

The requirement that each house maintain a record of its proceedings, or its work, was taken from the Articles of Confederation. Congress publishes two documents to fulfill this legal requirement. The journals make up the official record of all actions taken in the two chambers. However, the journals do not contain the debates that accompany actions taken by Congress.

During the first seventy-five years of the nation's history, the publication of congressional debates was random and incomplete. In the years from 1790 to 1825, House debates, but not Senate debates, were printed in some of the country's major newspapers. Beginning in 1834, several private companies published some debates and some newspapers and magazines published articles about Congress's activities. It was not until 1865 that *The Congressional Globe* began publishing all of the debates in both the House and Senate. When *The Globe*'s contract with the government ended in 1873, Congress provided that the United States Government Printing Office should have the sole responsibility for printing the daily proceedings of the national legislature. In fact, *The Congressional Record* has printed the complete record of proceedings each day that Congress has been in session since then.

Clause 4: The Independence of Congress

The fourth and final clause of Article I, Section 5, is similar in language to that found in the state constitutions of the 1780s. The Framers adopted it with very little debate. This provision, Clause 4, was designed to guarantee the independence of the legislative branch of government. It was intended to prevent a return to practices similar to those used by royal governors before the American Revolution. Those governors often had suspended and dissolved the popularly elected legislatures in the

filibuster prolonged floor debate aimed at defeating measures by preventing a final vote

cloture a procedure by which debate in the legislature is ended and an immediate vote is taken on the matter under discussion

Articles of Confederation the first constitution of the thirteen original United States; in effect 1781–1789

The Congressional Record has followed a standard format since its beginning. Two sections contain a record of the floor debates in each chamber. A third section permits members of Congress to add extensions to the remarks made during debates. These extensions often contain speeches given outside of Congress as well as newspaper and magazine articles. These are printed in the Extension of Remarks section of the *Record*. Because of this the *Record* has been called "the freest press in the world." *The Congressional Record* also includes a Daily Digest that prints the date and time of the next meetings of Congress and its committees.

ARTICLE I—House of Representatives; Members of Congress; United States Senate

Members of Congress
Norman Ornstein

vest to grant with particular authority, property, and rights

apportion divide proportionally or share according to a plan, such as representatives or taxes under a government

impeachment method by which the House of Representatives may charge the nation's highest-ranking officials, including the president, with wrongdoing; following impeachment, if the officials are found guilty of the charges, the Senate then may try them and remove them from office

colonies when their views opposed British policies. In fact, the Declaration of Independence listed royal interference with colonial assemblies as one of the grievances against the British monarch that justified the American Revolution.

ARTICLE I, SECTION 1, OF THE CONSTITUTION STATES

*All legislative Powers herein granted shall be **vested** in a Congress of the United States, which shall consist of a Senate and House of Representatives.*

ARTICLE I, SECTION 2, OF THE CONSTITUTION STATES

The House of Representatives shall be composed of Members chosen every second Year by the People of the several States, and the Electors in each State shall have the Qualifications requisite for Electors of the most numerous Branch of the State Legislature.

No Person shall be a Representative who shall not have attained to the Age of twenty-five Years, and have been seven Years a Citizen of the United States, and who shall not, when elected, be an Inhabitant of that State in which he shall be chosen.

*Representatives and direct Taxes shall be **apportioned** among the several States which may be included within this Union, according to their respective Numbers, which shall be determined by adding the whole Number of free Persons, including those bound to Service for a Term of Years, and excluding Indians not taxed, three fifths of all other Persons. The actual Enumeration shall be made within three Years after the first Meeting of the Congress of the United States, and within every subsequent Term of ten Years, in such Manner as they shall by Law direct. The Number of Representatives shall not exceed one for every thirty Thousand, but each State shall have at Least one Representative; and until such enumeration shall be made, the State of New Hampshire shall be entitled to chuse three, Massachusetts eight, Rhode-Island and Providence Plantations one, Connecticut five, New York six, New Jersey four, Pennsylvania eight, Delaware one, Maryland six, Virginia ten, North Carolina five, South Carolina five, and Georgia three.*

When vacancies happen in the Representation from any State, the Executive Authority thereof shall issue Writs of Election to fill such Vacancies.

*The House of Representatives shall chuse their Speaker and other Officers, and shall have the sole power of **Impeachment**.*

ARTICLE I, SECTION 3, OF THE CONSTITUTION STATES

The Senate of the United States shall be composed of two Senators from each State, chosen by the Legislature thereof, for six Years; and each Senator shall have one Vote.

Immediately after they shall be assembled in Consequence of the first Election, they shall be divided as equally as may be into three Classes. The Seats of the Senators of the first Class shall be vacated at the Expiration of the second Year, of the second Class at the Expiration of the fourth Year, and of the third Class at the Expiration of the sixth Year, so that one-third may be chosen every second Year; and if Vacancies happen by Resignation, or otherwise, during the Recess of the Legislature of any State, the Executive thereof may make temporary Appointments until the next Meeting of the Legislature, which shall then fill such Vacancies.

No Person shall be a Senator who shall not have attained to the Age of thirty Years, and been nine Years a Citizen of the United States, and who shall not, when elected, be an Inhabitant of that State for which he shall be chosen.

The Vice President of the United States shall be President of the Senate, but shall have no vote, unless they be equally divided.

president *pro tempore* (Latin, "for the time being") serving as president on a temporary basis

The Senate shall chuse their other Officers, and also a **President pro tempore**, *in the absence of the Vice President, or when he shall exercise the Office of President of the United States.*

The Senate shall have sole Power to try all Impeachments. When sitting for that purpose they shall be on Oath or affirmation. When the President of the United States is tried, the Chief Justice shall preside. And no person shall be convicted without the Concurrence of two thirds of the Members present.

indictment a formal written statement charging a person or persons with an offense after a grand jury has exammined the evidence and found that there is a valid case.

Judgment in Cases of Impeachment shall not extend further than to removal from Office, and disqualification to hold and enjoy any Office of honor, Trust, or Profit under the United States; but the Party convicted shall nevertheless be liable and subject to **Indictment**, *Trial, Judgment, and Punishment, according to Law.*

ARTICLE I, SECTION 4, OF THE CONSTITUTION STATES

The Times, Places, and Manner of holding Elections for Senators and Representatives, shall be prescribed in each State by the Legislature thereof; but the Congress may at any time by Law make or alter such Regulations, except as to the Places chusing Senators.

The Congress shall assemble at least once in every Year, and such Meeting shall be on the first Monday in December, unless they shall by Law appoint a different Day.

ARTICLE I, SECTION 5, OF THE CONSTITUTION STATES

*Each House shall be the Judge of the Elections, Returns, and Qualifications of its own Members, and a Majority of each shall constitute a **Quorum** to do Business; but a smaller number may adjourn from day to day, and may be authorized to compel the Attendance of absent Members, in such Manner, and under such Penalties, as each House may provide.*

quorum the number of members required to be present for a vote to take place

Each House shall keep a Journal of its Proceedings, and from time to time publish the same, excepting such Parts as may in their Judgment require Secrecy; and the Yeas and Nays of the Members of either House on any question shall, at the Desire of one fifth of those Present, be entered on the Journal.

Neither House, during the Session of Congress, shall, without the Consent of the other, adjourn for more than three days, nor to any other Place than that in which the two Houses shall be sitting.

ARTICLE I, SECTION 6, OF THE CONSTITUTION STATES

*The Senators and Representatives shall receive a Compensation for their Services, to be ascertained by Law, and paid out of the Treasury of the United States. They shall in all cases, except **Treason, Felony,** and **Breach of the Peace**, be privileged from Arrest during their Attendance at the Session of their respective Houses, and in going to and returning from the same; and for any Speech or Debate in either House, they shall not be questioned in any other Place.*

treason the offense of attempting to overthrow the government

felony a crime usually punished by death or a lengthy prison sentence

breach of the peace disturbance of the lawful or customary order and security within a community

emolument refers to profit or gain that an official may get, such as increases in salary and similar benefits

*No Senator or Representative shall, during the Time for which he was elected, be appointed to any civil Office under the Authority of the United States, which shall have been created, or the **Emoluments** whereof have been increased, during such time; and no Person holding any Office under the United States shall be a Member of either House during his continuance in Office.*

The Framers made Congress the first branch of government because they saw the two chambers of elected representatives as the heart of American democracy. Article I spells out the provisions for Congress. The Framers devoted as much detail in the Constitution to members of Congress as they did to any other matter, including the powers of the three branches of the government.

▲ "The Bulleys of the House"
Probably drawn by John L. Magee (1852?).

In Article I, Section 1, the Constitution gives all the legislative, or lawmaking, powers to the two houses of Congress. Sections 2 and 3 spell out the composition of the House of Representatives and the Senate, as well as the qualifications of their members. Section 4 gives the details of how senators and representatives are to be elected, and Section 6 discusses their rights.

The Constitution makes clear that the House and Senate are two different bodies. The different qualifications for members, constituencies, and methods of election reflect the different concepts the Framers had for the two houses. The House of Representatives, the "lower house," was to be closer to the people, and would thus more fully reflect their wishes and beliefs. The Senate, the "upper house," was to be more distant from public pressure, would represent the interests of the states, and act as a check on the House if it got carried away.

The House of Representatives

Members of the House of Representatives are elected more frequently, represent smaller voting districts, and their qualifications bring them closer to the people than members of the Senate. The most important difference lies in the methods of election to each body. The Constitution mandates that representatives be elected every two years. So in theory, all the members of the House could be replaced every two years. To qualify for the House, a representative must be at least twenty-five years old, a resident of the represented state, and a citizen for at least seven years.

Over the years, the courts have held that these are the only qualifications, and states have generally been barred from adding other requirements, in spite of ever-growing pressure to limit the number of terms Congress members may serve. States may not, in fact, bar felons from serving in the House (even though felons cannot vote!), nor can they require that a candidate for office live in that district (though most candidates usually do).

The Constitution, in Article I, Section 2, originally mandated that each House member represent about 30,000 people. The first House that met in 1789 had sixty-five members. As the United States grew in size and population, the number of representatives kept increasing. In 1929 Congress fixed the membership of the House at 435 members, and provided for the size of each congressional district and the number of representatives from each state to be adjusted after the population census taken every ten years.

During the second half of the twentieth century, western and southern states, such as Texas, California, and Florida, grew much faster than northeastern states, such as New York and Pennsylvania. Several states sued the federal government after the 1990 census, claiming that the census was inaccurate, undercounting many of their citizens, thereby causing them to lose representatives in the House. The Supreme Court ruled in favor of the federal government. Nevertheless, this issue has remained a difficult and partisan one.

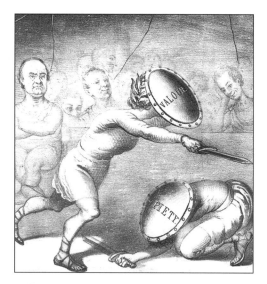

"The Gladiators of the Senate!"
Probably drawn by John L. Magee (1852?).

ratify to formally approve a document, thereby making it legal

The Senate

Membership in the Senate is not based on the census. Instead, each state elects two senators, each serving a six-year term. Only one-third of the senators stand for election each cycle, so the Senate cannot change dramatically even if the voters replaced all of them. The Framers intended this method of election to give the Senate a broader perspective and make it freer from public pressure than the House.

The qualifications that senators be at least 35 years old, live in their state, and be citizens for at least nine years also reflect the Senate's greater distance from the public. The Senate, like the House, also grew in size as new states joined the Union. The first Senate in 1789 had twenty-six members, representing thirteen states. At the end of the twentieth century, the Senate had 100 members to represent fifty states.

Originally, the Constitution did not call for the direct election of senators. Instead, it had state legislatures choose their state's senators, which also distanced senators from the public. But the Seventeenth Amendment, ratified in 1913, made the election process for senators more democratic by providing that voters in each state elect them directly. Although elections bring senators closer to the people, their six-year terms still make for a more deliberative body than the House.

The Senate is a unique part of the federal government. Since each state has two votes in the Senate but unequal population, some states that may not be large or seem politically important can wield very significant power. After the 1990 census, California had fifty-two representatives in the House and Wyoming had only one. Yet both states sent two senators. And if small states have senators with seniority, it often gives them great power, even compared to much larger states. In the 105th Congress that began in January 1997, Alaska was represented in the Senate by Senator Ted Stevens, chair of the powerful Appropriations Committee, and by Senator Frank Murkowski, chair of the important Energy and Natural Resources Committee.

Representatives at work in the House chamber below a gallery of spectators during a nineteenth-century session.

> The Framers intended that Congress serve as a forum for the interests that make up the nation. But what the legislator's job is has long been the subject of debate. Edmund Burke, a British political philosopher and member of Parliament in the 1770s, divided legislators into two groups. On one side are delegates who view their job as following public opinion and do what "the folks back home" want. The other group believes it was elected to lead and to work in the broader national interest. Burke called these legislators "trustees." Most members of Congress take this view. They agree with Burke, who said, "Your representative owes you, not his industry only, but his judgment, and he betrays instead of serving you if he sacrifices it to your opinion."

Congressional Rules and Benefits

Congress generally oversees its own affairs. In keeping with its power over congressional elections, it also judges their validity. Though states were given freedom to set the qualifications of office holders, Congress has always seated members, and in some cases has not seated the states' first choices. In the South during the Reconstruction years after the Civil War, Congress tightly monitored state elections, because of fears that still-powerful white Southerners would unfairly control elections. Again, during the civil rights era of the 1960s and 1970s, Congress closely watched the actions of Southern legislatures.

Members of Congress have many privileges, beyond receiving a salary. The Constitution protects all members from arrest when traveling to attend sessions or delivering speeches on the floor. Both houses of Congress restrict speaking on the floor to members, barring outsiders on all but a few occasions. Congress has many facilities for its members on Capitol Hill, such as a gym, medical clinic, and cafeteria. Because the Senate has fewer members than the House, senators also have more office space and generally larger staffs. This too shows that the two houses of Congress are quite independent of each other.

The Constitution does limit Congress members in some respects. They may not serve simultaneously in other branches of government. Members of Congress may not serve as judges, nor may they serve in foreign posts or accept titles of nobility, gifts, or offices from any foreign country without the consent of Congress.

Some of the benefits members of Congress enjoy—including their salaries—have always been controversial. One reason is that Congress sets its own pay. In 1789, it was five dollars a day for each day Congress was in session. When Congress increased it to six dollars a day in 1815, the public became outraged. Again, many years later, in 1989, when Congress voted itself another pay raise, a firestorm of protest swept the country. The Twenty-seventh Amendment, added to the Constitution in 1992, prohibits any sitting Congress from raising its own pay—any pay increase that Congress votes for can take effect only after another congressional election, thereby giving voters a chance to make their feelings known to their lawmakers.

see also

ARTICLE I—Congress; House of Representatives; Procedural Rules of Each House; United States Senate

★ Speech and Debate Clause

Jeffrey B. Morris

treason the offense of attempting to overthrow the government

felony a crime usually punished by death or a lengthy prison sentence

ARTICLE I, SECTION 6, CLAUSE 1, OF THE CONSTITUTION STATES

*The Senators and Representatives shall receive a Compensation for their Services, to be ascertained by Law, and paid out of the Treasury of the United States. They shall, in all cases, except **Treason**, **Felony**, and Breach of the Peace, be privileged from Arrest during their Attendance at the Session of their respective Houses, and in going to, and returning from, the same; and for any Speech or Debate in either House, they shall not be questioned in any other Place.*

The speech and debate clause protects members of Congress from being prosecuted or sued for their speeches or actions in enacting laws. This clause also has been held to protect persons who work for members of Congress or for congressional committees. However, the clause's protection does not apply to the speeches and actions that are not part of the lawmaking process, either by members of Congress or those who work for them.

The Precedents of Parliament

The speech and debate clause was not written into the Constitution just to protect individual members of Congress. It also was intended to safeguard Congress from the executive branch's using the courts to intimidate members. Thus, this clause is an important part of the constitutional system of checks and balances of power.

The Framers of the Constitution understood the centuries-long struggle of Parliament against England's monarchs. From the fourteenth to the seventeenth century, members of Parliament who spoke out against their rulers on such matters as the king's expenditures, issues of war and peace, and the succession to the throne, or who introduced bills the monarchs did not favor, feared the consequences of their actions. They knew that they might be arrested, imprisoned in the Tower of London, and even executed.

In 1641, King Charles I attempted to arrest five members of Parliament who opposed his policies. This action, which took place in Parliament, itself led to a bloody civil war in which King Charles I was defeated and put to death. After a long period of conflict and the overthrow of another monarch, the English Bill of Rights was adopted in 1688. It provided that "the Freedom of Speech, and Debate or Proceedings in Parliament, ought not to be impeached [interfered with] in any Court or Place out of Parliament."

Even after the English Bill of Rights was adopted, members of Parliament, during the eighteenth century, still could be punished for the crime of seditious libel. If convicted of this crime, members of Parliament could be imprisoned.

The colonists who fought for independence in the American Revolution were familiar with English history. They included in the Articles of Confederation a provision nearly identical to one in the English Bill of Rights: "Freedom of speech and debate in the legislature shall not be impeached or questioned in any court or place out of Congress." A few years later, the Framers included the speech and debate clause in the Constitution to strengthen the independence of the legislative branch of government.

Protection of Members of Congress

The speech and debate clause of the Constitution protects members of Congress from legal proceedings when they are involved with "legitimate legislative activity." This term refers to any activity that is essential to the

seditious libel the publication of material that encourages the disruption or overthrow of the government

Articles of Confederation the first constitution of the thirteen original United States; in effect 1781–1789

Senator William Proxmire issued a monthly Golden Fleece Award for the "biggest, most ironic, or most ridiculous example of wasteful public spending."

constituent a voter in a district who elects an official for representation

libel the publication of statements that wrongfully damage a person's reputation

Woodrow Wilson was a highly regarded scholar of government many years before he became president. In 1885 he wrote in *Congressional Government*: "It is the proper duty of a representative body to look diligently into every affair of government and to talk much about what it sees. It is meant to be the eyes and the voice, and to embody the wisdom and will of its constituents. . . . The informing function of Congress should be preferred even to its legislative function. . . . [I]nterrogated administration is the only pure and efficient administration. . . ."

ARTICLE I—Members of Congress

deliberations of Congress, such as delivering speeches on the floor of either chamber, speaking in committees, and committee reports and voting. Anything members of Congress say and do about legislative matters cannot be used as evidence in any criminal prosecution, nor can members be sued for these things. Moreover, the courts cannot punish members of Congress for their motives in speaking or casting votes. The Supreme Court has ruled, for example, that the chair of a Senate committee who allegedly conspired with state officials to violate a person's civil rights could not be sued over it.

However, not every action of a member of Congress is "privileged," or protected by the speech and debate clause. Members are not protected when they make speeches in other places outside Congress. They can be sued, for example, for what they say in campaign speeches, in press releases, and for what they do when serving their **constituents**. The Supreme Court ruled in *Hutchinson* v. *Proxmire* (1979) that while press releases are "valuable and desirable" ways of informing the public, they are not "essential to the deliberations [debates] of the legislative body." In this case, a senator claimed that a scientist had wasted public funds, but the senator did so in a press release, not in a speech on the floor of Congress. In this case, the scientist was able to sue the senator for **libel**.

Protection Against Criminal Prosecution

The speech and debate clause can sometimes even mean that a member of Congress can commit a crime and not be arrested or tried in court. In one example, a member accepted a bribe for making a speech on the floor of Congress. In that case, *United States* v. *Johnson* (1966), the Supreme Court ruled that the clause meant that the member of Congress could not be examined in court about the speech itself. However, in another case involving a senator who accepted a bribe intended to influence the performance of his legislative duties, the Court held that this member could be prosecuted. In that ruling, *Brewster* v. *United States* (1971), Chief Justice Warren Burger wrote, "Taking a bribe is, obviously, no part of the legislative process or function; it is not a legislative act." The fact that the senator took a bribe meant that he could be prosecuted, even though he could not be held accountable for the legislative act that the bribe was intended to influence. Thus, a member of Congress cannot avoid prosecution for taking a bribe.

In 1972, the Supreme Court held, in *Gravel* v. *United States*, that a senator could not be prosecuted for reading into the public record a committee documents that the federal government had classified as secret. However, it also ruled that the senator involved could be prosecuted for the way he obtained these materials and for his attempts to find a publisher to print them. In this same decision, the Court held, for the first time, that the speech and debate clause also protects persons who work on Congress members' staffs and persons working for congressional committees. The justices reasoned that because the legislative process has become so complex, the day-to-day work of congressional staffs is "so essential to the Member's performance" that the clause also protects these aides. In this way, the independence of Congress is further ensured.

★ Emoluments
William Lasser

No Senator or Representative shall, during the Time for which he was elected, be appointed to any civil Office under the Authority of the United States, which shall have been created, or the Emoluments whereof shall have been increased, during such time; and no Person holding any Office under the United States shall be a Member of either House during his continuance in Office.

ethics high standards of honest and honorable dealing

Clause 2 of Article I, Section 6, is known as the ineligibility clause or the emoluments clause. The clause was intended to prevent corruption. Its purpose was to take away any financial reason for members of Congress to create new government positions or to raise the salary or benefits of existing offices, since any members of the Congress passing such legislation would be ineligible to serve in such offices until after their congressional terms had ended. The ineligibility clause was an early example of a congressional ethics rule. It was inspired by the Framers' distrust of politicians as well as their desire to prevent the kind of corruption they saw among members of the British Parliament.

The Impact of the Clause

Unfortunately, the ineligibility clause has had little impact on government. For one thing, as Justice Joseph Story noted in his commentary on the Constitution in 1833, this provision does not get at the heart of the problem. The clause does not bar a member of Congress for life from serving in offices created or whose salary and benefits were increased during his or her time in office. It bars the member from such offices only "during the time for which he was elected." So members of Congress who are nearing the end of their time in office could serve in a newly created position as soon as the current Congress ends, perhaps a matter of mere weeks or months. Even more serious, members of Congress would be under the greatest temptation to take part in such arrangements at the end of their terms if they had not been reelected and needed continued employment.

The ineligibility clause deals with an unlikely situation. For true corruption to take place, the entire membership of Congress would have to vote for a measure that would benefit at most a few members. What is far more likely to happen is that members of Congress might be tempted by the president to exchange a vote or several votes in return for an executive appointment. The ineligibility clause does nothing at all to prevent this possibility.

Problems Involving the Clause

Even though the emoluments clause is not very useful, it has sometimes proved to be annoying. On several occasions, a member of Congress who was qualified for an executive or judicial post ran into difficulty because the salary or benefits of the office had recently been increased. In general, Congress has responded in such cases by withdrawing the increase that it had granted earlier for the office. Such action does not satisfy a strict

A 1953 cartoon satirizing the political dangers for members of Congress who wish to legislate salary increases for themselves, an activity typically unpopular with voters.

When Hugo L. Black sat on the Supreme Court for the first time on October 4, 1937, two members of the bar stood up five times in all to claim that he was seated illegally. One of them, Albert Levitt, had brought suit just after the Senate had confirmed Black. The other, Patrick Kelly, said he would now bring suit. This was "an extraordinary situation," he said. Chief Justice Charles Evans Hughes cut him off, warning Kelly not to talk further. Any motion would have to be submitted in writing to the clerk, Hughes said. It would then be taken under advisement. Kelly wrote it out and handed it to the clerk. The Court quickly dismissed both motions the next time it sat.

ARTICLE II—Appointments

The Legislative Process
Robert J. Spitzer

revenue income from investments, salary, or property; a goverment's sources of revenue include taxes and licenses

interpretation of the provision, since the benefits of office *had* been increased during the nominee's service in Congress, even if the emoluments were later reduced. But withdrawing the increase satisfies the spirit of the law and has raised no legal difficulties.

In 1909, Congress repealed a 1907 salary increase for the secretary of state in order to allow President William Howard Taft to appoint Senator Philander C. Knox to that office, since Knox had been a member of the Senate when the salary increase was adopted. In 1975, Congress took similar action, repealing an automatic cost-of-living adjustment to allow President Gerald Ford to name Senator William Saxbe as attorney general. Neither of these cases caused a controversy and no legal objections were raised.

Two private citizens filed a lawsuit in the Supreme Court in 1937 opposing the appointment of Hugo Black as an associate justice of the Supreme Court on the grounds that Congress had recently approved an increase in the retirement benefits of federal judges. Black had left the Senate to join the Court. The Court dismissed this legal claim on technical grounds. Political objections to Black's appointment were met with the argument that he would not be eligible for the increased emolument for at least nineteen years.

ARTICLE I, SECTION 7, OF THE CONSTITUTION STATES

All Bills for raising **Revenue** *shall originate in the House of Representatives; but the Senate may propose or concur with Amendments as on other bills.*

Every Bill which shall have passed the House of Representatives and the Senate shall, before it becomes a Law, be presented to the President of the United States: If he approves he shall sign it, but if not he shall return it, with his Objections, to that House in which it shall have originated, who shall enter the Objections at large on their Journal, and proceed to reconsider it. If, after such Reconsideration two thirds of that House shall agree to pass the bill, it shall be sent, together with the objections, to the other House, by which it shall likewise be reconsidered, and if approved by two thirds of that House, it shall become a Law. But in all such Cases the Votes of both Houses shall be determined by Yeas and Nays, and the Names of the Persons voting for and against the Bill shall be entered on the Journal of each House respectively. If any Bill shall not be returned by the President within ten Days (Sundays excepted) after it shall have been presented to him, the Same shall be a Law, in like Manner as if he had signed it, unless the Congress by their Adjournment prevent its Return, in which Case it shall not be a Law.

Every Order, Resolution, or Vote to which the Concurrence of the Senate and House of Representatives may be necessary (except on a question of Adjournment) shall be presented to the President of the United States; and before the Same shall take Effect, shall be approved by him, or being disapproved by him, shall be repassed by two thirds of the Senate and House of Representatives, according to the Rules and Limitations prescribed in the Case of a Bill.

The first paragraph of Article I, Section 7, ensures that the House of Representatives has more power over money bills, including bills to raise taxes, than does the Senate. The Framers of the Constitution specified this since the House is closer to the people than the Senate. Representatives in the House are elected more often—every two years—and elected directly by the people. Senators are elected every six years. Originally, state legislatures elected senators until the Seventeenth Amendment, added to the Constitution in 1913, provided that they, too, are to be elected by the people.

Presidential Power in Spending

Even though the power of the purse—the power to appropriate (set aside) and spend federal money—rests with Congress, the president has some authority over expenditures. Presidents and leaders of Congress realized early in the nation's history that presidents needed some power to alter spending authorized by Congress. For example, in 1803, President

In 1878, Congress passed the silver bill over the president's veto.

In 1947 Congress passed the Taft-Hartley Act. This act restricts organized labor's power to strike, outlaws the closed shop (which required that employers hire only union members), and introduces a sixty-day "cooling off" period before a strike or lockout can begin. Taft-Hartley also gives the government the power to obtain a court order to prevent any work stoppage that would "imperil the national health or safety." Outraged union leaders said it was a "slave labor bill," "**fascistic**," and "conceived in sin." President Harry Truman vetoed it, calling it an attack on the worker. But both houses of Congress overrode his **veto** the same day. The bill became law and remains on the books, basically unchanged, at the end of the twentieth century.

fascistic showing a tendency toward or real demonstration of strong autocratic or dictatorial control

veto refuse to sign a bill into law

Thomas Jefferson decided not to spend the $50,000 that Congress had authorized for the purchase of gunboats for the navy, because circumstances had changed. Rivalry with France over control of land west of the Mississippi River had eased. When the United States purchased this region from France in 1803, the need for gunboats seemed to end.

Jefferson's actions did not mean that he was trying to oppose the will of Congress or overturn an appropriation bill. He simply wanted to avoid spending money if it was unnecessary to do so. This practice by presidents not to spend money that Congress sets aside for a certain purpose is called "impoundment." Jefferson's impoundment did not last long, however. After studying the matter for another year, he decided to use the money to buy the gunboats.

President Nixon's Impoundments

American presidents often have impounded funds for reasons of efficiency or to prevent wasteful spending. Congress usually has accepted this practice when the president used it to save money. However, this kind of informal impoundment changed during the presidency of Richard M. Nixon. In 1972 and 1973, President Nixon impounded large appropriations of federal funds, more than any president ever had done. Congress had voted these funds to pay for such programs as emergency federal loans, environmental protection, supplying rural electricity, public housing projects, and sewer construction. In one instance, Nixon impounded half of an $18 million appropriation for a clean water project.

Nixon's impoundments were challenged in court. Congress and others argued that these impoundments were really attempts by the president to change national policy, not to increase efficiency. The federal courts heard nearly eighty cases challenging Nixon's impoundments and ruled in all but three of them against the president's actions.

President Nixon's excessive practice of impounding funds led Congress to enact the Impoundment Control Act of 1974, which ended the old impoundment practice, substituting two new procedures: deferrals and rescissions. A "deferral" is a proposal from the president to Congress to delay spending federal funds. A "rescission" is a proposal from the president to Congress to cancel the expenditure of funds. In both cases, the president must obtain Congress's approval in order to delay or cancel federal spending.

The President's Role in Lawmaking

The final step in the legislative process is set forth in the second paragraph of Section 7. After both houses of Congress pass a bill in identical form, the bill goes to the president. This action, called "presentment" or "presentation," ensures that the president has a final opportunity to review all legislation before it becomes law. In this review, the president

Important laws are often enacted despite a president's veto. Here are some examples. In 1947, over President Truman's veto, Congress passed the Taft-Hartley Act restricting organized labor's right to strike. In 1973, Congress enacted the War Powers Resolution over President Nixon's veto. This act limited the president's authority to commit American troops to fight in a foreign conflict without congressional approval. In 1974, over President Ford's veto, Congress passed the Freedom of Information Act, allowing the public more access to government documents.

has four options, or choices. First, the president may approve the bill and sign it into law within ten days (not counting Sundays) of receiving it. Second, if the president has objections to the bill, he may veto it by returning the bill to the house where it began. This action is sometimes called a "return" veto or a "regular" veto.

Veto power. If the president uses the veto, he must include a written message outlining his objections to the bill. Congress may then attempt to override the president's veto, a procedure that requires a two-thirds vote in both houses of Congress. History has shown that this is difficult to achieve. Nearly 93 percent of all presidential vetoes have been sustained—that is, not overridden by Congress.

The president's third option when reviewing a bill passed by Congress is to take no action. If the president does not sign the bill or veto it, the bill automatically becomes law after ten days (not counting Sundays), just as if the president has signed the bill. However, presidents rarely choose this option, since in most cases they either favor or oppose a bill.

"Pocket veto." The fourth option occurs only when presidents want to veto a bill when Congress is about to adjourn, or end its last session. In this case, the president may exercise a "pocket veto" simply by not signing the bill. Since Congress has adjourned, it cannot consider the bill again, and the legislation dies.

The Framers gave the president the pocket veto to prevent Congress from misusing the return veto procedure. It is important to remember that when presidents exercise a return veto, Congress must be able to receive the returned bill. The Framers of the Constitution were afraid that Congress might try to prevent a presidential veto by passing a bill it knew the president would want to veto, and then quickly adjourn so that the president could not return the vetoed bill. Since without the bill's return there can be no veto, the bill would then become law after ten days, with or without the president's signature. The president can use the pocket veto only when Congress has finished its work and adjourned for the last time until the newly elected Congress takes office.

In the second half of the twentieth century, both Congress and the president have designated individuals to act for them at certain times in the legislative process. In this way, bills passed by Congress and vetoed bills can be transmitted between the two branches if the president is out of town or if Congress has recessed for a holiday or a long weekend.

Political cartoonist Clifford K. Berryman's commentary on the running battle between Congress and the presidency over such issues as taxes. This cartoon appeared in 1943, when wartime decision making required speedy cooperation between Congress and the White House.

Balancing Congressional and Presidential Power

These complicated procedures for handling bills were designed to strike a compromise between executive and legislative power. As the first branch of government, Congress is given the final say through its ability to override a presidential veto. But the two-thirds vote required to override the veto forces Congress to seriously consider the President's objections to a bill.

Some of the Framers of the Constitution, such as Alexander Hamilton, had proposed that the president be given an absolute veto—that is, a

Political cartoon depicting President Andrew Jackson as an absolute monarch who abuses his veto power and tramples on the Constitution.

veto Congress could not override, but a majority of the Framers rejected this idea. They believed that it was too similar to the hated absolute veto power of British monarchs. While the pocket veto is, in effect, an absolute veto, the limitations on its use underscore the Framers' desire not to give the President too much power over legislation.

The veto power also is a key example of the checks and balances written into the Constitution. Not only was it considered a vital tool to prevent Congress from encroaching on the President's power, but it was also seen as an important instrument to block laws that were not well thought out or that might be unconstitutional. The veto thus was viewed as a positive element in lawmaking because it allowed the President to bring a bill back to Congress for a final round of debate and deliberation. Moreover, the veto power highlights the fact that the lawmaking power is clearly shared by the legislative and executive branches of government.

Early American presidents used the veto cautiously. From the first veto by President George Washington in 1792 until 1868, presidents vetoed eighty-eight bills. Since that time, presidents have vetoed over 2,000 bills. President Franklin D. Roosevelt holds the record for the most vetoes, at 635. President Grover Cleveland averaged the most vetoes per year. He vetoed 584 bills during his two terms, for an annual average of 73. Seven presidents never vetoed a bill. They were John Adams, Thomas Jefferson, John Quincy Adams, William Henry Harrison, Zachary Taylor, Millard Fillmore, and James A. Garfield. Through the 1970s and 1980s the veto continued to be a vital presidential tool. Presidents Gerald Ford and George Bush, for example, used the veto, as well as the threat of a veto, as an effective weapon in their arsenal of powers to control the flow of legislation.

Exceptions to the Rule

The third and final paragraph of Section 7 was added to make sure Congress did not try to bypass the president. For example, in an attempt to avoid a veto, Congress might call the same bill by another name when presenting it to the president. Tricks like these had been tried by colonial legislatures to avoid vetoes by British governors.

There are a few exceptions to Section 7's requirement that "Every order, resolution, or vote" in Congress be presented to the president. Amendments to the Constitution, which require a two-thirds vote in both houses, do not require presidential approval. (The procedures for constitutional amendments are described in Article V of the Constitution.) Congress also may enact congressional resolutions, which are passed by a simple majority vote, without the president's approval. Congressional resolutions are not bills proposed to become laws. Instead, they express Congress's opinion on a subject, or "sense of Congress," and are not legally binding. In addition, congressional votes on its own administrative matters need not be presented to the president either.

★ The Unwritten Constitution in Congress

Norman Ornstein

faction a party or group united by a common cause

Federalist advocating a strong, central government of separate states and of the adoption of the U.S. Constitution

Anti–Federalist member of the group opposing the adoption of the U.S. Constitution; favored states' rights and argued successfully for the Bill of Rights

president *pro tempore* (Latin, "for the time being") serving as president on a temporary basis

sergeant-at-arms an officer of Congress who preserves order and executes commands

The Constitution rarely spells out the way the institutions it created should be organized and operate. Article I, which sets up the legislative branch of government, gives more detail than most of the other articles. It outlines the membership, qualifications, powers, elections, and limits on the legislative branch. In contrast, Article II, which creates the presidency (the executive branch), and Article III, which establishes the courts (the judicial branch), provide fewer such details.

But Article I tells little about how Congress would actually run itself. Still, the Constitution gives Congress a great deal of power over itself. It can choose its own leaders, set its own rules, regulate the conduct and ethics of its members, and fix the pay and benefits of its officers, members, and their staffs. Congress also has the power to settle disputes arising out of its elections.

Political Parties

When the first Senate and House of Representatives met in 1789, they organized themselves in ways that the Framers had not expected. In particular, and almost from the start, Congress organized around political parties, even though political parties are mentioned nowhere in the Constitution.

Political parties developed from two **factions** that held differing opinions when the Constitution was adopted. The **Federalists** supported the Constitution, with its strong central government, while the **Anti-Federalists** wanted less power concentrated in a national government and more of a role for the states.

Previous allies in the revolutionary cause became bitter political enemies when the government sat down to do its work. These two factions soon became the majority and minority political parties that struggled for control in elections to Congress and the presidency. Over the next two centuries, these differences evolved into the Democratic and Republican parties. But the initial framework, with majority and minority parties as basic building blocks, is not radically different from what it was in the early era of congressional history.

The parties reflected differences in political beliefs, values, policies, and regional interests. Organizing around the two parties became a convenient way for members of Congress to organize debate and dissent, and to do business as well as reflect voter choices. In modern times, the two parties play an extensive role in Congress. The leadership of the House and the Senate is organized along party lines. Each house has majority and minority leaders as well as other party officers. The positions of Speaker of the House and **president *pro tempore*** of the Senate (the senior member of the majority party), officers mentioned in the Constitution, are not technically party posts, but in practice they are extensions of the majority party and the persons who hold them are members of it.

The majority party leaders in Congress appoint other congressional officers, such as the **sergeants-at-arms**, the clerk of the House, and the secretary of the Senate. They play an important role in running the legislative branch, from controlling action on the floors of both houses to setting the rules for members' restaurants. The Senate majority leader has special power to be recognized to speak on the Senate floor at any time and to shape the Senate's agenda and schedule. Even though the Senate majority leader usually consults the minority party leaders, the majority leader has the main responsibility.

Political Parties and Congress

Political parties are not unique to America. In fact, they are central forces in every democratic nation. The role of the parties differs with the political system. Some countries have **proportional representation** in their national legislatures. In Israel, when a political party wins 10 percent of the votes in an election, it gets 10 percent of the total number of seats in the Knesset, Israel's legislature. This kind of proportional representation usually results in many political parties, because a party does not have to win a majority of votes in an election in order to send representatives to the legislature or to have important political power.

The United States does not have proportional representation. All members of Congress are elected by the voters. The 435 seats in the House of Representatives and the 100 seats in the Senate are filled by the candidates who win elections in their districts or states—that is, the candidate who wins the most votes or more than 50 percent of the votes, depending on the state's election rules. This method of electing members to Congress is sometimes called a "first-past-the-post" system. It almost always makes sure that the two-party system continues, since no party can win representatives if its candidates do not get 50 percent of the votes (at least in some districts or states). Even if smaller parties won 10 percent of the vote in every congressional district, none of their candidates could be seated.

Another difference between the United States and other democratic nations is that most of them have parliaments, not congresses. Great Britain, which has a parliament, has no separation of powers between the

proportional representation the basing of the number of seats that each political party wins in the legislature on the number of votes it receives in an election

House Speaker Newt Gingrich and Senate Majority Leader Robert Dole took over both houses of Congress in 1995.

In a 1965 speech, U.S. Congressman Joseph W. Barr described the American legislative system in the following way:

"We live in a world of specialists. While the congressional system with its high degree of specialization [the committee system] may appear fragmented and disorderly to those who admire the symmetry of the parliamentary system, I would submit that the congressional system is peculiarly adapted to the world we live in today."

"The political party having the majority ... [will] necessarily control all the committees ... because they ... must, as a party, protect themselves against the chance of the control of the business of the body going into the hands of their opponents."

—James A. Bayard, Jr. (1799–1880) U.S. Senator, quoted in *The Congressional Globe* (1857).

executive and the legislature. The Framers' dislike of the British Parliament's great power led them to create the system of separation of powers. In a parliamentary government, the prime minister, who is the chief executive, is also the leader of the legislature. The powers of the legislative and executive branches are joined. The majority party controls parliament by having its members vote together on almost every issue. Thus, the government's actions are viewed as the actions of the party in power. If the majority party's members do not act together, the government can fall from power, and new elections must be held.

In the United States, the power of the majority political party is not as clear cut, nor is there such tight unity among its members. One party may be the majority party in the House while the other is in the majority in the Senate. One party may have a majority in both houses of Congress, while the president is a member of the other party. Party members are independent and free to vote as they or their constituents want. Both Republicans and Democrats in Congress tend to vote for the issues supported by their party, but it is not unusual for them to vote with members of the other party.

Committees in Congress

Both houses of Congress organize themselves around committees as well as parties. Even though the Constitution makes no mention of committees, Congress had to find a way to operate efficiently. Within a few years after Congress first met, it became apparent to members that setting up small groups to handle each bill they considered was not very efficient. Some of the subjects Congress considered, such as taxes, spending, tariffs, foreign affairs, and military forces, would need regular attention. So Congress created a system of permanent committees to handle these areas. Over the next two centuries, the committee system changed periodically, from many committees to fewer, and then back again.

Since the end of World War II, the House and the Senate have each added about one hundred subcommittees to the fifteen to twenty full standing committees in each house. Even so, the observation President Woodrow Wilson made when he was a professor of political science remains largely true today: "Congress on the floor is Congress in public exhibition; Congress in its committees is Congress at work."

The committees divide by party into majority and minority. The chairs, or leaders, of the committees are always from the majority party. During the latter part of the nineteenth century, when the House had very strong speakers who controlled Congress, the Speaker chose the chairs directly. Chairmen who did not reflect the Speaker's views or obey his orders were not chairmen for long. In 1910 members of the House rebelled against this kind of control. A new method of choosing the chairs developed—the seniority system. By unwritten rule, members who had served on particular committees longest automatically became chairs. Party members vote every two years to select chairs, who are still the most senior members of Congress. The Speaker of the House plays a major role, and occasionally will make a less-senior figure a chairperson.

The membership of most committees reflects each party's strength in Congress. If the Senate has fifty-five Republican senators and forty-five Democrats, membership on its committees will be about 55 percent Republicans and 45 percent Democrats. One exception is the ethics committee, the panel each house sets up to investigate charges of violations of the rules or standards by members. By tradition these groups have an equal number of members from each party.

▶ The Senate Ethics Committee during hearings on the savings and loan affair (1990). This is the only congressional committee where both parties are represented equally.

constituency the collective body of voters in a district which elects an official for representation

filibuster prolonged floor debate aimed at defeating measures by preventing a final vote

Congressional committees resemble "little legislatures." Appointment to them is a matter of urgent concern both to members of Congress and to their political parties. Senator Bill Bradley said "there were fierce battles" within the Democratic Steering Committee, which assigns senators to committees. "The battles are generally drawn along classic lines—liberal/conservative, environment/industry, rural/urban, East/West." The chairman of the committee is usually, but not always, its most senior member. In 1995 House Speaker Newt Gingrich named several committee chairs who were not the most senior members of their committees. "I thought they would bring a level of aggressiveness and risk-taking that we would need in these very important positions," Gingrich said.

The House and the Senate Compared

Although both the House of Representatives and the Senate operate in similar ways, they nevertheless differ in important aspects. The Constitution creates two distinct institutions in size, **constituency**, qualifications of members, powers, as well as other features. The rules of the bodies reflect some of these differences. Most important are the role of the Rules Committee in the House and the use of the **filibuster** in the Senate. The much larger House cannot operate effectively without highly structured, formal rules for handling debates and voting. The House Rules Committee acts as a "traffic cop," regulating the time spent on every bill, and the number and structure of amendments that may be considered. To limit debate, the House has a five-minute rule, a time limit for members to speak. Also, any amendments to bills that members propose must be germane—they must concern the bill's subject matter. This is how the Rules Committee works to speed up the action on bills so as to reflect the will of the majority of members. Representatives often find their own freedom and roles subordinated to the interests of the House.

The Senate rules on scheduling, amending, and debating bills are much less strict. As a smaller, more informal body, it is very sensitive to the rights and viewpoints of all its members, including those of the minority party, and considers its members' right to be heard more important than reaching a decision that reflects the will of the majority. Thomas Jefferson, George Washington, and the other Framers regarded the Senate as the body that would be more removed from public pressures than the House, whose members, with smaller constituencies and two-year terms, were closer to the voters. The Framers believed that the Senate would be more sensitive to protecting minorities from the tyranny of the majority.

The rules of the Senate reflect that view. The Senate has no five-minute rule and no rule that amendments must be germane. It usually operates through unanimous consent and has a filibuster tradition. Sometimes, senators use this right to debate with no time limit to delay or prevent a vote on a bill they oppose. Under contemporary rules, it takes sixty senators—far more than a majority—to stop the debate and bring a matter to a vote. The use of the filibuster and the difficulty in ending one reflect the Senate's role as a protector of minority views. It also shows that the Senate, unlike the House, often places the rights of its individual members above the interests of the Senate as a whole.

ARTICLE I—Congress; House of Representatives; Organization of Congress; United States Senate

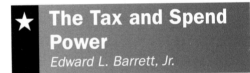

The Tax and Spend Power
Edward L. Barrett, Jr.

duty a tax on goods brought into the country

impost an imposed charge; a tax or duty

excise a tax that a government puts on the manufacture, sale, or use of a domestic product

Articles of Confederation the first constitution of the thirteen original United States; in effect 1781–1789

ARTICLE I, SECTION 8, CLAUSE 1, OF THE CONSTITUTION STATES

*[The Congress shall have the Power] to lay and collect Taxes, **Duties**, **Imposts** and **Excises**, to pay the debts and provide for the common Defense and General Welfare of the United States, but all Duties, Imposts and Excises shall be uniform throughout the United States.*

A major weakness of the Articles of Confederation was that Congress had no power of taxation. Congress could only request that the states contribute their fair share to the national treasury. It had no power to collect taxes when, as often happened, the states did not provide funds. Article I, Section 8, of the Constitution remedied this by granting Congress the power to levy and collect taxes.

The Power to Tax

The power of taxation has raised many questions throughout the nation's history. What is the scope of Congress's power to tax? Are there limitations on this power beyond the requirement that taxes be uniform throughout the country? Can Congress use its taxing power to regulate? For example, a national tax of one dollar on a pack of cigarettes will raise revenue, but it also will probably reduce the number of people who smoke. Does it make a difference if Congress states in its tax law that the purpose of a tax is to regulate? Again, in the case of the cigarette tax, what if Congress stated as part of this tax law that its purpose is to end the sale of cigarettes, even if the tax itself produces very little revenue? Can Congress regulate matters not within its enumerated powers by using its power to tax?

enumerated powers the powers listed in a constitution; these powers also are sometimes called the *expressed* powers

The early years. This issue of taxation and regulation had considerable significance in the nation's early years. In that period, the scope of the federal government's power to regulate directly was limited. However, by the end of the twentieth century, its regulatory power had vastly increased, and the importance of this issue had greatly diminished. This development is clearly seen in a review of several key decisions of the Supreme Court.

In the early 1900s, the Supreme Court upheld the taxes to regulate passed by Congress. In *McCray* v. *United States* (1904), for example, the Court ruled that even though Congress had no power to forbid the sale of colored margarine, it could impose a high tax on this product even if this tax had the effect of preventing its sale. However, some years later, the Court found other regulatory acts unlawful. In *Hammer* v. *Dagenhart* (1918), a federal statute forbidding the interstate transportation of goods made by child labor was not upheld. The Court ruled that Congress had exceeded its power to regulate under the commerce clause. Congress then attempted to regulate by taxation. It imposed a 10 percent tax on the annual net profits of manufacturers that employed children under certain ages. Again, the Supreme Court overruled Congress. In the *Child Labor Tax Case* (1922), the justices declared that this tax was, in fact, a

Political cartoon showing Uncle Sam collecting checks from tax evaders.

regulation: "[A] court must be blind not to see that the so-called tax is imposed to stop the employment of children. . . . It is prohibitory and the regulatory effect and purposes are palpable."

The Supreme Court's 1950 opinion. By mid-century, however, the Court once more upheld taxes passed by Congress for regulatory purposes. In *United States* v. *Sanchez* (1950), the justices upheld a tax on narcotics that required taxpayers to register with the federal government. The Court said: "It is beyond serious question that a tax does not cease to be valid merely because it regulates, discourages, or even definitely deters the activities taxed . . . or the revenue purpose of the tax may be secondary. . . . Nor does a statute necessarily fall because it touches on activities which Congress might not otherwise regulate." However, even though the Court's ruling in the *Child Labor Tax Case* may still be good constitutional law in defining when a tax ceases to be a tax and becomes a regulation, it is of minor importance. Now Congress almost always has the power to regulate, and it can cast its regulation in the form of a tax.

The Power to Spend

The Constitution states that Congress may tax "to pay the debts and provide for the common Defense and general Welfare of the United States." The Framers of the Constitution debated the scope of Congress's power to spend. James Madison argued that Congress could spend money only to carry out its other powers. He declared that providing for the general welfare did not grant Congress any additional power. In contrast, Alexander Hamilton stated that the general welfare clause granted Congress a substantive power to tax and spend, as long as it was doing so for the general welfare of the United States.

***United States* v. *Butler*.** In the early twentieth century, this issue grew in importance because Congress began providing funds to the states on condition that they agree to carry out certain activities—activities that were beyond the direct power of Congress to regulate. Because of technical limitations on standing to sue (the right of a person or a group to bring a lawsuit in court), the issue did not come before the Supreme Court until 1936. The justices reviewed the matter in *United States* v. *Butler* (1936). The *Butler* case reviewed the provisions of the Agricultural Adjustment Act of 1933. This law involved an agreement between the Secretary of Agriculture and American farmers by which farmers reduced the acreage they planted in exchange for payments from the federal government. The money for these payments was raised by a tax levied on the processors of various crops; in fact, all of the proceeds from the tax on processors were to be used to pay the farmers.

Alexander Hamilton's legacy. The Court's reasoning in *Butler* was clearly set forth. First, it held that the processors on whom the tax was levied had standing to sue, because they were required to pay a substantial tax earmarked for the spending being challenged. Next, the Court adopted Hamilton's view that the power to spend could be exercised for the general welfare and was not limited to direct grants of power to Congress. Finally, the Court ruled that it was not required to decide whether the spending in this case was for the general welfare. It was not required

statute a law enacted by the legislative branch of government

▲ Senator William Roth of Delaware protested the high costs government is charged by defense contractors at a 1985 news conference.

In 1791 Secretary of the Treasury Alexander Hamilton submitted a Report on Manufactures. His goal was to stimulate industry in the new country. He listed seventeen industries but did not mention milling, even though flour had long been a major export. Hamilton proposed a system of tariffs for industry, awards for agriculture, and a network of internal improvements under federal sponsorship. He argued that the taxing and spending clause gave Congress a separate, additional power to act for the general welfare. This view remains one of the major interpretations of the tax and spend power.

Article I—Fiscal and Monetary Powers

to do so because the law involved was a regulation, not an expenditure, and was invalid because it went beyond Congress's regulatory power.

The Supreme Court's adoption of Hamilton's position in its decision in *Butler* soon became its basis for upholding expenditures by Congress. In *Helvering* v. *Davis* (1937), the Court upheld the Social Security Act of 1935, ruling that expenditures for old-age pensions was spending for the general welfare. In *Buckley* v. *Valeo* (1976), the Supreme Court held that expenditures of funds to finance presidential campaigns were lawful expenditures for the general welfare. And in *South Dakota* v. *Dole* (1987), the Court upheld a congressional statute withholding five percent of federal highway funds from any state that permitted the sale of alcoholic beverages to persons under the age of twenty-one. The justices declared that even if Congress had no power to directly regulate legal drinking ages, it could act indirectly under its spending power to encourage states to adopt uniform laws on this matter.

Federal grants of funds to state and local governments have now become important regulatory tools. Those expenditures have increased dramatically, from less than $11 billion in 1965 to an estimated $228 billion in 1995. At the same time, however, the constitutional issues involved have lost their former importance. If expenditures are said to be for the general welfare, the intrusion of the federal government into a local area no longer matters. Because Congress's powers to spend for the general welfare and to regulate under the commerce clause are now so broad, any constitutional challenge to such federal spending is unlikely.

No major constitutional problems exist with Congress's power to tax and spend. Congress exercises such broad regulatory powers that it no longer needs to get around limitations on these by attempting to use taxing and spending powers. Instead, Congress uses regulatory powers as handy ways of achieving its goals. The most important limits here are political considerations.

Borrowing Money
Sheldon Goldman

Articles of Confederation the first constitution of the thirteen original United States; in effect 1781–1789

government-guaranteed financially backed so that the government assures the security of a bond, treasury note, etc.

ARTICLE I, SECTION 8, CLAUSE 2, OF THE CONSTITUTION STATES

[The Congress shall have the Power] to borrow money on the credit of the United States.

The power to borrow money is an essential power of government. Without the ability to borrow, government could not function. The Framers of the Constitution granted Congress this broad power because of the hardships the national government had faced lacking this authority under the Articles of Confederation. The power to borrow money, as authorized by the Constitution, gives Congress the right to sell government-guaranteed securities such as bonds, treasury notes, and bills. The Constitution places no limit on Congress's exercise of this power.

revenue income from investments, salary, or property; a government's sources of revenue include taxes and licenses

federal deficit the amount of money borrowed to make up the difference between money that is spent and what has been earned

national debt the total amount of money owed by a nation; it is made up of the federal deficit plus the interest owed on the money that has been borrowed by the indebted country

interest money paid by a borrower to a lender for the use of borrowed money

deficit spending spending funds in excess of income, especially by a government

legal tender money which can be legally offered to pay a debt and which the person or institution who is owed the money must accept

Under the gold standard, the basic unit of currency is equal in value to a specific amount of gold and can be exchanged for that amount. The gold standard was the first formal international monetary system of modern times. It came into effect during the late nineteenth and early twentieth centuries. Gold served as an instrument of exchange and as the only standard of value until the international gold standard broke down in 1914. Several systems replaced it before most countries accepted a system of controlled floating gold rates in the 1970s that lessened the importance of gold in international dealings. This system remained in effect at the end of the twentieth century.

The Power to Borrow

In theory, Congress can borrow any amount of money for any purpose it chooses and specify any provisions it wishes for repaying this debt. Likewise, the Constitution does not place any limit on the amount of debt the government can owe. In practice, however, use of the borrowing power has major political and policy consequences. Thus, if the federal government spends more than the revenue it takes in, it must borrow to make up the difference, creating a federal deficit. If the annual federal government budget continues to be out of balance, the deficit increases and the national debt grows. Yet the more money the government borrows, the larger the amount of interest it owes on this debt. The federal government then must borrow more money to pay the interest owed on the money it has already borrowed. Congress routinely passed laws placing a ceiling on the national debt. Then just as routinely it raised the debt limit when political pressures seemed to leave it with no other practical course of action.

During the 1980s and early 1990s, the national debt reached historic highs. Some critics said it was reaching a crisis level. Politicians of both major parties condemned deficit spending and warned that the bloated federal debt of several trillion dollars was a crushing burden being passed along to future generations of Americans.

Finally, in the late 1990s, Congress and the executive branch imposed limits on federal spending and began to reduce the size of government. These balanced budget agreements were to continue for several years. In addition, the nation's prosperous economy produced increased revenues for the federal government. As a result, a dramatic reduction took place in the annual federal deficit. If balanced federal budgets continued, it was hoped, this would also lead to a lowering of the national debt. However, it was clear that reducing government spending and the size of the federal deficit would require a continuing political struggle.

The Power to Regulate Currency

Congress's power to borrow money has been dealt with in only a few Supreme Court decisions. *Hepburn* v. *Griswold* (1870) involved federal finances during the Civil War. As part of its effort to pay for the Union's war effort, Congress passed the Legal Tender Act. That measure authorized the federal government to issue greenbacks, a new currency not backed by gold. The federal government made greenbacks legal tender, or lawful currency, for all debts, both public and private. Thus, all private and public debts that persons owed before the Civil War now could be repaid in greenbacks if those debts simply specified repayment in lawful currency. However, greenbacks were worth much less than the gold-backed dollars those persons had borrowed.

The Legal Tender Act and its later amendments were challenged before the Supreme Court. In *Hepburn* v. *Griswold*, the justices ruled, by a 4-to-3 vote, that it was unconstitutional to require that greenbacks must be accepted as lawful currency in payment of debts from the years before the act was passed. However, the *Hepburn* decision was extremely unpopular and threatened to ruin many Americans. This ruling meant that businesses would be forced to repay their debts with the older, more expensive currency backed by gold.

Soon after this, two new justices who supported the greenbacks joined the Court. When the Court then heard a second legal tender case, it reversed its earlier decision. In the *Legal Tender Cases* in 1871, by a 5-to-4 vote, the Court declared that Congress has a wide array of powers it may use to justify issuing greenbacks and making them lawful currency. Among the powers it named was the power to borrow money. Nevertheless, the following year the Court also ruled on the question of repaying debt contracts in gold-backed currency. The Court decided that creditors could not be forced to accept an amount in greenbacks that was worth less than gold dollars. As a result of the Court's decision in *Trebilcock* v. *Wilson* (1872), most creditors who made loans insisted on gold clauses in their contracts of debts. Similarly, when the federal government borrowed money by issuing bonds, it too included gold clauses promising repayment in hard currency.

Later Supreme Court Decisions

This promise to repay bonds containing gold clauses became an issue during the Great Depression of the 1930s, when the federal government went off the gold standard. The Supreme Court heard two cases involving these gold-clause bonds. The main case concerned a business-issued bond. In a 5-to-4 vote, the Court upheld the government's right to regulate currency and denied the bondholder's claim.

The second case, however, involved the gold clause in a government bond. These were the facts in the Court's decision in that case, *Perry* v. *United States*. In 1918, John M. Perry had bought a government bond that required the government to repay both the principal and interest in gold-backed currency "of the present standard of value." Then fifteen years later, during the Great Depression, the federal government sought to devalue the currency. Among other measures, the government no longer repaid its bond debt in currency redeemable in gold.

Perry argued that when the government had borrowed the money, it had promised to repay it in gold. He insisted that this promise was superior to the power of Congress to regulate the value of currency. In its *Perry* decision, eight justices of the Supreme Court agreed with Perry on this point. However, by a 5-to-4 vote, the justices also ruled that Perry had not proved "actual damages" since gold was no longer currency and the nation's economy had adjusted to the standard of the new currency. In fact, these justices pointed out that Perry had not shown he suffered "any loss whatsoever," and satisfying his claims would be "an unjustified enrichment."

Congress soon passed a law prohibiting such lawsuits against the government. Thus, even if bondholders could prove monetary losses, they had no legal recourse. This demonstrates that, in practice, then, Congress can set any terms it wishes for repaying what it borrows. Furthermore, it can use its power to regulate the value of currency to repay such loans in whatever form it wishes. The power to borrow money on the credit of the United States is indeed an awesome power.

creditor person to whom a debt is owed

gold clause language included in a contract promising the repayment of debts in gold or in a hard currency amount equal to its value in gold

bond note, usually from a corporation, stating that a debt for a certain amount is owed; the note also contains a promise to pay back interest on the amount at a certain rate, as well as to pay the loan amount (principal) by a certain date

devalue lessen, reduce, or cancel the worth of something

recourse alternate choice or plan of action

★ Commerce Clause: Through the Nineteenth Century
Lino A. Graglia

Articles of Confederation the first constitution of the thirteen original United States; in effect 1781–1789

tariff tax or duty on imported goods

enumerated powers the powers listed in a constitution; these powers also are sometimes called the *expressed* powers

▲ A worker weighs gold ingots inside the Federal Reserve Bank.

[The Congress shall have the Power] To regulate Commerce with foreign Nations, and among the several states, and with the Indian Tribes.

This provision is one of the most important clauses in the Constitution, for two reasons.

First, one of the major defects in the system of government under the **Articles of Confederation** was that Congress had no power to regulate interstate trade (trade between the states). The thirteen states had passed **tariff** laws and put up other trade barriers. These had prevented the new nation from creating a unified, prosperous economy. The need for a central government with power to remove these barriers to trade and to create a national market was the main reason Alexander Hamilton and James Madison led the movement for the national convention that wrote the Constitution.

Second, the power to regulate interstate commerce has proved to be an extremely broad power. It is probably the most important and most frequently used power that Congress has. The interstate commerce clause has been the basis for federal regulations on an almost endless range of subjects. Along with Congress's power to tax and spend, the commerce power has had enormous consequences. It has changed the national government from a government of limited, **enumerated powers**—powers mostly involving commerce and defense—into a government with authority to legislate on all issues, including key social policy issues that affect people's daily lives.

Gibbons v. *Ogden* Decision

The most important Supreme Court decision on the meaning of the commerce clause is *Gibbons* v. *Ogden*. This 1824 decision marked the Court's first full review of the commerce clause. The *Gibbons* case involved a New York law that gave Aaron Ogden the exclusive right to operate steamships in New York Harbor between New York and New Jersey. When Thomas Gibbons began competing with Ogden, Ogden sued. A New York state court then ordered Gibbons to stop operating steamships in New York Harbor.

Gibbons argued that the New York law was unconstitutional because the commerce clause did more than grant Congress the power to regulate interstate commerce. It also prohibited the states from enacting laws that affected commerce between the states. This idea came to be known as the "negative" or "dormant" commerce clause doctrine. Chief Justice John Marshall's opinion for the Court agreed that this doctrine was a strong argument, but he decided the case on different grounds. He ruled that the New York law was unconstitutional because it conflicted with a federal law that authorized Gibbons to operate steamships in interstate trade.

Chief Justice Marshall defined the commerce power in very broad terms. "Commerce," he wrote, meant not only buying and selling things

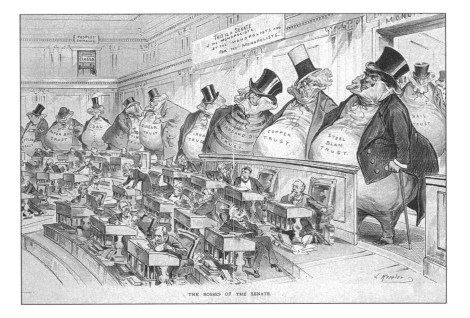

Cartoon illustrating the power of industry at a time when Congress attempted to regulate the economy. The sugar, steel, oil, and copper lobbies are depicted as giants looming over the legislators.

Chief Justice Marshall was sharply criticized for his decision in *McCulloch* v. *Maryland* in 1819. The Democratic-Republican supporters of Jefferson, Madison, and Monroe protested that his ruling trampled states' rights. They charged that it "murdered" the spirit of the Constitution. Yet Marshall's 1824 decision in *Gibbons* v. *Ogden* came to be known as "the **emancipation** proclamation of American commerce." By the end of the nineteenth century, the Supreme Court had removed almost all regulations from American businesses.

emancipation freedom from another's control, restraint, or bondage

but included all forms of "commercial intercourse." He further stated that Congress could regulate all commerce that "affects more states than one." This meant that Congress could regulate all commercial activities except those "which are completely within a State, [and] which do not affect other States." Marshall declared that this power "is complete in itself, may be exercised to its utmost extent, and acknowledges no limitations other than are prescribed in the Constitution." He strongly hinted that there were no limits on the commerce power that a court could enforce, and that the scope of the power was solely for Congress to decide.

Supreme Court Rulings After *Gibbons*

During most of the nineteenth century, commerce clause cases did not involve the question of the scope of the power of Congress. Instead, the cases involved the "dormant" commerce clause doctrine. That is, what limits, if any, did the commerce clause place on the power of the states? In 1851, in *Cooley* v. *Board of Wardens,* the Supreme Court reached a compromise position on this question. It held that the commerce clause did not totally prohibit, though it limited, the states' power to enact laws affecting interstate commerce. State laws are permitted here, the Court ruled, if they concern only local matters. But state laws are prohibited if they concern matters where a uniform national rule is required.

The *Daniel Ball* case in 1871, which involved the scope of Congress's commerce clause power, illustrates the difficulty of separating what is "interstate" from what is not. The question before the Court was whether the *Daniel Ball,* a steamship operated solely within the state of Michigan, was subject to regulation by Congress under the commerce clause. In its decision, the Supreme Court held that Congress had the power because the steamship carried goods that came from out of state and would be carried to other states by other carriers. Therefore, the steamship was operating in interstate commerce and subject to federal regulation.

monopoly the situation that exists when only one person or company sells something in any given area

INTRODUCTION—Constitutional Concepts; Constitutional Origins;
ARTICLE I—Commerce Clause: The New Deal; The Tax and Spend Power

★ Commerce Clause: The New Deal
Barry Cushman

Congress's Power Under the Commerce Clause

The great importance of the commerce clause became clear during the late nineteenth century, when Congress began to use it to regulate the nation's economy. Congress passed the Interstate Commerce Act in 1887 to regulate railroad rates. It also passed the Sherman Antitrust Act in 1890 to prohibit business **monopolies** and business combinations in restraint of trade.

In the first Supreme Court case involving the Sherman Act, *United States* v. *E.C. Knight & Co.* in 1895, the justices saw that the commerce clause could easily become all-powerful despite the intent of the Constitution. The Court attempted to limit this power by defining "commerce" very narrowly. Manufacturing, the Court ruled, was not commerce, even though manufactured products were to be shipped to other states. Congress could not prohibit sugar manufacturers from combining to form a monopoly. The result was that Congress was powerless to prevent a business monopoly that could control the price and the amount of sugar sold throughout the United States.

Later courts rejected this attempt to limit the commerce power by using a narrow definition of "commerce." With few exceptions, courts returned to the broad meaning adopted by Chief Justice Marshall in the *Gibbons* case. Under this definition, Congress could regulate any activity, even local, that "was in the stream of" or that "affected" interstate commerce. This means that Congress can regulate anything that affects the movement of goods or people from state to state or that affects out-of-state commercial activity. Because almost anything can have such an impact, the commerce clause power has turned out to be extremely broad. Indeed, it seems there is almost no subject, from health to morality, that Congress cannot regulate under the commerce power.

ARTICLE I, SECTION 8, CLAUSE 3, OF THE CONSTITUTION STATES

[The Congress shall have the Power] To regulate Commerce with foreign Nations, and among the several States, and with the Indian tribes.

During the nineteenth century, Congress seldom exercised its exclusive power to regulate interstate commerce, or commerce between the states. Yet the Supreme Court often struck down state and local laws that interfered with the commerce clause. Strictly applying this clause would have invalidated many state laws. To avoid this, the Court decided on a compromise: State laws that directly affected interstate commerce were unconstitutional, but state laws that indirectly affected it were allowed.

Is Commerce "Local" or "National"?

As Congress began using its commerce power more often in the late nineteenth century, the justices applied the same thinking to federal laws

President Roosevelt whips Congress and the nation along the road to emergency legislation in a 1930s political cartoon.

that they had applied to state laws in commerce clause cases. In *United States* v. *E.C. Knight* (1895), the Court ruled that Congress could not prevent sugar refiners from joining their companies together to form a monopoly. The Court pointed out that the "national" activities of commerce were separate from "local" activities like manufacturing, declaring that "manufacturing precedes commerce, and is not part of it." The justices said that even though this merger would probably affect commerce, the effect would be only "indirect." They concluded that Congress could regulate a local activity only if its effect on commerce was "direct."

At the same time, the Supreme Court approved federal regulation of local activities. The *Shreveport Rate* case of 1914 involved a federal regulation of a railroad company's rates for service between two cities in Texas. Because this travel took place entirely within one state, it seemed to be a local matter. Nonetheless, the Court ruled that sometimes local railroad rates had a "close and substantial" relationship to interstate commerce. In those cases, the Court held, the federal government could regulate the rates.

The Court also permitted federal regulation of business dealings in public stockyards on the ground that such dealings were in a "stream of interstate commerce." Livestock came from the western states to the stockyards, where they remained briefly to be fattened and then sold. Then the livestock again moved across state lines to butchers and customers in eastern states. The Court reasoned that because Congress could regulate the entire flow of this business "stream," it could regulate local activities that took place within it.

Yet such interstate commerce cases were narrow exceptions to the general rule that only states could regulate local activities. The due process clause of the Fifth Amendment generally limited the types of businesses that Congress could control. Until the mid-1930s, all of the "close and substantial" cases in which local activities directly affected interstate commerce involved railroad regulation. All of the "stream of commerce" cases concerned either stockyards or grain exchanges.

Regulation During the New Deal

During the Great Depression of the 1930s, the federal government tried to solve the country's economic problems by regulating more local activities than ever before. One of the centerpieces of President Franklin D. Roosevelt's New Deal was the National Industrial Recovery Act (NIRA). NIRA imposed "codes of fair competition" that regulated the production and sale of goods in various industries. The Schechter brothers, kosher butchers in New York, were charged with violating several provisions of NIRA's Live Poultry Code, including selling a chicken not fit for consumption. In 1935, in *Schechter Poultry* v. *United States,* which became known as the "sick chicken case," the Supreme Court struck down this code. The justices ruled that the stream of commerce had ended because the Schechters sold all their chickens for local markets in New York. Thus, their activities affected interstate commerce only indirectly. This decision by the Court killed the NIRA.

The next year, the Court struck down the Guffey Coal Act, which regulated working conditions of coal miners. In *Carter* v. *Carter Coal Co.* (1936), the justices said that because the coal in this case had not started its movement in interstate commerce, the stream of commerce had not yet begun. Therefore, job conditions at this coal mine affected interstate commerce only indirectly.

The Court-Packing Plan and Its Effect

These and other decisions by the Supreme Court frustrated President Roosevelt, who complained that the Court was trying to take the country back to a "horse and buggy" era definition of interstate commerce. In February 1937, soon after winning a landslide reelection, he announced a plan to add six new justices to the Court, saying that the justices then on the bench were too old and unable to keep up with their workload. Everyone knew that the president's real purpose was to have a majority on the Court who would vote to uphold New Deal laws.

Congress never approved President Roosevelt's "Court-packing" plan. But while the Senate was considering it, the Supreme Court upheld the National Labor Relations Act, a key New Deal measure. This act required employers and labor unions to bargain over wages, hours, and working conditions rather than go out on strikes that could harm the economy. The government lawyers who brought the cases to court were careful to select companies that got their raw materials from outside their states and then sent finished products across state lines for sale. These companies, they argued, were in a stream of commerce. In *NLRB* v. *Jones & Laughlin Steel Corp.* (1937), the Court held that Congress could regulate labor relations at a steel plant because they had a "close and substantial" relationship to interstate commerce.

In one of his popular fireside chats, President Franklin D. Roosevelt addressed the issue of the Supreme Court's opposition to his New Deal program. "We cannot yield our constitutional destiny to the personal judgement of a few men who, fearful of the future, would deny us the necessary means of dealing with the present," he said.

Cartoon showing the Democratic donkey kicking up a storm in opposition to President Roosevelt's 1937 Supreme Court reform plan.

The Increased Scope of Federal Regulation

During the late 1930s, the Supreme Court upheld congressional regulation of even more local activities on the ground that they had a "close and substantial" relationship to interstate commerce. The Court was able to do so because it no longer used the Fifth Amendment's due process clause to limit the kinds of businesses that Congress could regulate. The Court used the *Shreveport* case as a model for regulating local sales of farm products like milk and tobacco.

By the early 1940s, however, the Court no longer used the "close and substantial" test or the "stream of commerce" doctrine. Many of the older justices began to retire in 1937, and by 1941 President Roosevelt had appointed a majority of the justices. These new justices did not believe in the distinction between direct and indirect effects on commerce.

The Supreme Court upheld federal regulation of workers' wages in a lumber mill in *United States* v. *Darby Lumber Co.* (1941). This decision reversed the Court's 1936 ruling in the *Carter Coal* case. Then, in *Wickard* v. *Filburn* (1942), the Court approved a federal law penalizing a farmer for planting wheat on his farm without the government's permission. The farmer had not sold the wheat but used it only to feed his livestock and his family. But the Court ruled that if many farmers did the same, it would have a substantial effect on interstate commerce. Thus, by the end of the New Deal, it seemed that there was almost nothing that Congress could not regulate under its commerce power.

In February 1937, President Franklin D. Roosevelt proposed an increase in the size of the Supreme Court. He recommended that one additional justice be appointed for every member of the Court over the age of 70, up to a total of 15 members. The reason he gave for this proposal was to make the Court more efficient. But he was frustrated that the Court had overturned much New Deal legislation—thirteen laws over the previous two years alone. (This compared to only two laws between 1789 and 1865, and even 58 between the Civil War and the New Deal.) FDR's opponents immediately called the plan "Court-packing," and it aroused intense opposition. Despite the President's popularity, the proposal failed as the Court began to uphold important New Deal laws. Roosevelt later said that he lost the battle but won the war.

★ Commerce Clause: After the New Deal
Deborah Jones Merritt

ARTICLE I, SECTION 8, CLAUSE 3, OF THE CONSTITUTION STATES

[The Congress shall have the Power] To regulate Commerce with Foreign Nations, and among the several States, and with the Indian tribes.

Since the end of the New Deal in the late 1930s, the Supreme Court has put few limits on Congress's power to regulate "Commerce . . . among the several States." Instead, the Court has confirmed its decisions expanding the commerce clause during the New Deal, and has continued to recognize the need for national regulation of complex social and economic problems.

Broad Scope of the Commerce Clause

In 1964, in *Katzenbach* v. *McClung,* the Court upheld Title II of the Civil Rights Act of 1964. That act prohibited racial discrimination in hotels, restaurants, and other public facilities. The case involved a family-owned restaurant, Ollie's Barbecue, in Birmingham, Alabama. Although the restaurant served mostly local customers, it purchased nearly half of its food from out of state. The Court ruled that this connection with interstate commerce, or commerce among the states, was reason enough to allow the federal regulation imposed by the Civil Rights Act.

65

James Brady, a former White House secretary shot during an assassination attempt against President Reagan, looks on as President Clinton signs the Brady Handgun Violence Prevention Act (1993). The bill, which required a five-day waiting period and a police background check on handgun buyers, was thrown out by the Supreme Court in 1997.

The Supreme Court's *Katzenbach* decision not only affirmed Congress's broad power to legislate under the commerce clause, it also began a new era of civil rights enforcement. Ollie's Barbecue had refused to serve African Americans in its dining room from the day it began business in 1927. Many other restaurants and hotels had followed similar practices, and most state governments had not taken strong actions to end such discrimination. By upholding the Civil Rights Act, the Supreme Court now allowed Congress to attack discrimination nationwide.

The Court's *Katzenbach* ruling also made it clear that Congress, rather than the Supreme Court, is the main judge of whether an activity involves interstate commerce. If Congress determines that conduct like discrimination affects the nation's economy, the Court will uphold this view, as long as some reasonable grounds exist to support it. Congress, therefore, has broad authority to decide which problems require national attention.

Limits on the Commerce Clause

For nearly thirty years, the series of rulings by the Supreme Court from the New Deal era through its *Katzenbach* decision suggested that Congress could regulate any activity under the commerce clause. If Congress could control the sale of barbecued ribs at a small, family-owned restaurant in Alabama, why could it not use the commerce clause to regulate any local activity?

The *Lopez* Case. In 1995 the Supreme Court made it clear that the commerce clause still places some limits on congressional power. The Court, in *United States* v. *Lopez,* struck down the Gun-Free School Zones Act. This law had banned the possession of any gun within 1,000 feet of any school. But in enacting this legislation, Congress had not made any findings to show a connection between gun possession and interstate commerce. In fact, during the hearings on the bill, Congress had seemed to ignore questions raised about its commerce clause authority, brushing aside the comments of two witnesses on that issue.

Because of these facts, the Supreme Court, in its *Lopez* decision, held that Congress had not shown that the possession of guns near schools has a large effect on interstate commerce. Despite this, the justices acknowledged, as they had in previous cases, that Congress has the power to determine if any activity has such an effect. The Court declared that it would uphold any finding by Congress of a large effect if the finding is reasonable. The unusual circumstances of the *Lopez* case had led the Court to invalidate the gun possession law.

Consequences of *Lopez*. The *Lopez* decision encouraged many individuals to challenge a variety of federal laws as being outside Congress's power, most of which the courts had rejected. Most constitutional law scholars believe that *Lopez* places only a narrow restraint, or limit, on congressional power. It requires Congress to be careful to recognize the limits on its commerce power and to provide evidence showing that a regulated activity substantially affects interstate commerce. As long as Congress follows these guidelines, the Court probably will uphold federal laws based on the commerce clause.

▶ From its first location in Des Plaines, Illinois, the McDonald's fast-food chain has expanded to become a national enterprise. Restaurants as vehicles of interstate commerce must abide by all laws, including those that ban discrimination.

Other Limits on the Commerce Clause?

The Supreme Court has imposed one other limit on the Congress's power under the commerce clause. The Court has held that Congress may not use that clause to issue direct commands to state and local governments. Congress may override state laws by passing federal laws on any subject that substantially affects interstate commerce. It also may persuade state and local governments to cooperate with federal programs by offering them federal funds for such cooperation. But Congress may not simply order state and local governments to act as agents of the federal government.

In 1993, for example, Congress passed the Brady Handgun Violence Prevention Act. That law required handgun dealers to collect information from those who wished to buy handguns and then wait five days before selling them the guns. During this waiting period, government officials were to check buyers' backgrounds to make sure they were qualified to purchase these weapons.

Clearly, Congress has the power to regulate handgun sales in this way. Firearms are part of the national economy, and their sale "substantially affects" interstate commerce. In *Printz* v. *United States* (1997), the Supreme Court ruled that Congress had gone too far when it ordered local police to make the required background checks. The Court declared that Congress could hire its own sheriffs to check buyers' applications, or it could offer federal funds to the states if their own sheriffs checked the applications, but, the Court added, Congress could not simply order state employees to carry out a federal law.

The guidelines set forth by the Supreme Court in its *Printz* decision ensure that state governments keep some independence from Congress. Congress retains ample power to achieve its goals under the commerce clause. Since *Printz,* for example, many state governments have voluntarily continued to perform background checks, and Congress has worked to create a national checking system.

Some legal experts thought that *United States* v. *Lopez* would be "the opening cannonades of a constitutional revolution," while others were doubtful. The case has reminded Congress that it has no general power to regulate whatever it thinks is in the public interest. Justice Stephen Breyer pointed out in his dissenting opinion that if Congress wants to make it a federal crime to possess a gun in a school, it must make the case that "gun-related violence near the classroom poses a serious economic threat" to interstate commerce. Congress did not do this, but it could easily do so. If it did, that law would likely be constitutional under the *Lopez* standard.

In addition to granting Congress power to regulate commerce "among the several States," the commerce clause gives Congress authority to regulate commerce "with the Indian tribes." This part of the commerce clause has caused less controversy than its use in interstate commerce. The Supreme Court has given state governments little power in regulating Indian tribes, granting that power solely to Congress or to the tribes themselves.

In summary, the commerce clause gives Congress broad power to regulate subjects "substantially affecting" interstate commerce. The modern Supreme Court has placed only modest limits on Congress's power under this clause. This approach has allowed Congress to deal with problems requiring national attention, while preserving the authority of state governments to handle local problems.

★ Citizenship and Naturalization
Peter J. Spiro

naturalization becoming a citizen

alien citizen of another country

naturalization laws laws that set requirements to be fulfilled for becoming a citizen

immigration coming to a country where one is not a native, usually to settle there; in this context, it refers to deciding who may be physically admitted into and removed from the United States

Articles of Confederation the first constitution of the thirteen original United States; in effect 1781–1789

ARTICLE I, SECTION 8, CLAUSE 4, OF THE CONSTITUTION STATES

[The Congress shall have the Power] To establish an uniform rule of Naturalization, and uniform Laws on the subject of Bankruptcies throughout the United States.

The naturalization clause gives Congress the power to determine what requirements aliens must meet in order to become citizens of the United States. Under this provision, Congress has passed naturalization laws without much constitutional controversy since the early days of the Republic. But the Supreme Court has set strict limits on the federal government's power to deprive Americans of their citizenship.

The federal government's power to regulate immigration also is based in part on the naturalization clause. Under the plenary (complete) powers doctrine, the courts have been unusually willing to allow the political branches to regulate immigration. The courts also have consistently upheld federal laws that discriminate against aliens in public benefits and jobs.

Qualifications for Citizenship

The Framers adopted the naturalization clause to prevent states from setting their own qualifications for national citizenship. The Articles of Confederation had made the states responsible for naturalization. One of the Framers, Roger Sherman of Connecticut, explained that, rather, the federal government "should have the power of naturalization, in order to prevent particular States receiving citizens, and forcing them upon others who would not have received them in any other manner." If states had kept the power of naturalization, any one state could harm the whole nation by granting citizenship to persons whom other states might not consider worthy of the status.

The first laws. Congress passed the first naturalization law in 1790. That law provided that persons "of good moral character" who had resided for at least two years in the United States were eligible for citizenship upon taking an oath to support the Constitution. In 1795, Congress amended the oath to require persons applying for naturalization to give up their former citizenship. The infamous Alien and Sedition Acts of 1798 briefly extended the residency requirement to fourteen years. In 1802, it was reduced to five years, a requirement that still applies in most cases.

For many years, naturalization was restricted on the basis of race. The 1790 law allowed only "free white persons" to become citizens. In 1870, persons of African ancestry also became eligible for naturalization. In 1882, Congress passed a law expressly making Chinese aliens ineligible for citizenship. In 1922, the Supreme Court's decision in *Ozawa* v. *United States* established that Japanese persons were not "white" and therefore could not become naturalized citizens. These racial qualifications were not completely eliminated until 1952.

The Fourteenth Amendment. Citizenship may be obtained by birth as well as by naturalization. Birthright citizenship was historically subject to racial qualifications. In *Dred Scott* v. *Sandford* (1857), the Supreme Court had ruled that black persons could not hold U.S. citizenship. The Fourteenth Amendment, adopted in 1868, overruled *Sandford,* and provided that all persons born in the United States are citizens at birth.

In *United States* v. *Wong Kim Ark* (1898), the Supreme Court ruled that the citizenship clause of the Fourteenth Amendment applied to persons born to aliens living in the United States. Since then, this decision has been interpreted to give citizenship even to children of aliens who enter or remain in the United States in violation of immigration laws. But in the late twentieth century, birthright citizenship became a controversial political issue. Constitutional amendments have been proposed to halt the granting of birth citizenship to the children of undocumented aliens, but Congress has not adopted any of these proposals.

The Loss of Citizenship

expatriation the loss of citizenship

Before the twentieth century, expatriation was not regulated by federal law. During the eighteenth and nineteenth centuries, state laws and practices by the federal executive branch regulated expatriation. This usually meant that American citizens, both native born and naturalized, would lose their citizenship if they became naturalized citizens of another country. Naturalized American citizens could lose their citizenship if they returned to live in the country of their birth. These rules were included in the first federal law on expatriation, which Congress adopted in 1907.

Expatriation. Later court rulings expanded the grounds for expatriation. The federal government could take away citizenship if an American citizen served in the military forces, held political office, or voted in the election of another country, or if a citizen was guilty of deserting the armed forces of the United States. In 1958, in *Trop* v. *Dulles*, the Supreme

"Once let the black man get upon his person the brass letters, U.S.—let him get an eagle on his button, and a musket on his shoulder, and bullets in his pocket, and there is no power on earth which can deny that he has earned the right to citizenship."

—Frederick Douglass (1817–1895), American abolitionist and writer.

Гостиница „МЕТРОПОЛЬ"
г. Москва

▲ Lee Harvey Oswald, the presumed assassin of President John F. Kennedy, requested in this letter dated October 31, 1959, that his American citizenship be revoked.

Court struck down the loss of citizenship for deserting the American armed forces as cruel and unusual punishment. But in a related case, *Perez* v. *Brownell* (1958), the Court, in a 5-to-4 decision, upheld the forced expatriation of an American citizen who had voted in a Mexican election.

Voluntary revocation. Less than ten years later, in *Afroyim* v. *Rusk* (1967), the Court reversed its position and overruled the *Perez* decision. Justice Hugo Black, who wrote the Court's opinion, strongly denied that Congress had the power to "rob a citizen of his citizenship," asserting that citizenship could be lost only when it was "voluntarily relinquished." This practice, still in effect at the end of the twentieth century, means that the federal government can take away a person's citizenship only when that person specifically requests that the government do so.

One result of the *Afroyim* decision and later cases is that the United States has come to allow dual citizenship. A United States citizen may hold citizenship in both the United States and another country, as, for example, in the country where a person's grandparents were citizens. American citizens can become naturalized in other countries without fear of losing their United States citizenship. But people from other countries who become naturalized American citizens still are required to renounce, or give up, their former citizenship. The renunciation oath, however, has never been enforced.

Immigration Regulation

The naturalization clause also has been interpreted as the basis for federal control over immigration. In the nation's early years, immigration was regulated by state laws that often applied to citizens as well as aliens. Many states, for example, limited or barred the entry of criminals, the poor, or the sick, regardless of their citizenship. In a series of decisions in the late nineteenth century, however, the Supreme Court prohibited the states from regulating the entry of aliens.

In the *Passenger Cases* (1849), the Court first struck down a state tax on incoming aliens as a violation of the commerce clause. In *Chy Lung* v. *Freeman* (1875), the Court overturned a California statute that denied Chinese immigrants entry into the United States. This and later Court decisions stressed that immigration involves relations with other nations, and therefore should be a matter of exclusive federal regulation.

The Supreme Court struck down state laws on immigration at the same time that it applied a very relaxed standard in the review of federal immigration laws. In the 1880s and early 1890s, Congress passed a series of acts known as the Chinese exclusion laws. Under these laws, alien Chinese workers who had left the United States were denied permission to return to their established U.S. residence, and also deported from the country without hearings if they could not prove a legal residence.

The Chinese exclusion laws were ruled constitutional in a series of cases. In *Fong Yue Ting* v. *United States* (1893), the Court found that aliens seeking admission or resisting expulsion were not entitled to due process, because these actions did not involve a deprivation of liberty within the meaning of the Fifth Amendment.

▶ Immigrants becoming American citizens at a naturalization ceremony.

Although the target of harsh criticism, the Court remained tolerant of immigration measures that would be found unconstitutional in other contexts. For instance, aliens can be prevented from entering the United States on the basis of views that would otherwise be protected by the First Amendment. Aliens also may be denied entry or deported on the basis of confidential information not revealed to them. As the Court stated in *United States ex rel. Knauff* v. *Shaughnessy* (1950), "[w]hatever the procedure authorized by Congress is, it is due process as far as an alien denied entry is concerned." The Court reaffirmed in *Fiallo* v. *Bell* (1977) that "over no conceivable subject is the legislative power of Congress more complete than it is over the admission of aliens."

Discrimination Against Aliens

As it has done in its rulings on immigration, the Supreme Court has limited the ability of state governments to discriminate against noncitizens. As early as 1886, the Court struck down a San Francisco ordinance discriminating against laundries run by Chinese aliens. Then, in a series of decisions starting with *Sugarman* v. *Dougall* (1973), the Court found aliens to be a "suspect class" for purposes of the Fourteenth Amendment's equal protection clause. This determination allows the Court to closely examine state laws that are discriminatory. As a result, the Court has overturned state laws prohibiting aliens from becoming state civil servants, lawyers, engineers, and public notaries.

But the Court has ruled that states are allowed to discriminate against aliens when a state benefit involves a political function. Thus,

ordinance law

public notary an officer or other person who certifies that deeds, contracts, and other writings are real and not false or imitated

A desire to limit "foreign" influences has long been part of American culture. In 1880 San Francisco passed a law that made it a crime to operate a laundry in any building not made of stone or brick. The law was aimed at wooden laundromats run by persons of Chinese descent. It allowed officials to make exceptions, but they denied all two hundred applications made by persons of Chinese ancestry while granting all eighty applications made by Caucasians. In *Yick Wo* v. *Hopkins* (1886), the Supreme Court ruled that this law violated the Fourteenth Amendment's equal protection clause.

see also

FIRST AMENDMENT—Seditious Libel; EIGHTH AMENDMENT—Cruel and Unusual Punishment

aliens may be denied the right to vote in state and federal elections, even though such aliens often had voted in the nineteenth century. On this basis, the Court has upheld state laws that made aliens ineligible to be public school teachers and police officers.

In contrast, the Court has allowed the federal government much greater authority to discriminate against aliens when public benefits are involved. Although the justices struck down an Arizona law that placed a residency requirement on aliens for receiving welfare benefits in *Graham* v. *Richardson* (1971), five years later the Court upheld a similar requirement that Congress had imposed for federal welfare benefits. The issue of whether aliens are eligible for public assistance benefits probably will be reviewed in future cases, because Congress passed welfare laws in the late 1990s that expressly give state governments the options to discriminate against aliens.

Constitutional issues relating to immigration and naturalization have become matters of growing interest both to the American public and to lawmakers. The courts, too, are likely to reexamine the constitutional conflicts raised by immigration and naturalization law.

★ Bankruptcy
Lawrence P. King

naturalization becoming a citizen

debt an obligation to pay money or goods to another person

creditor person to whom a debt is owed

debtor a person who owes something, such as money or goods, to someone else

ARTICLE I, SECTION 8, CLAUSE 4, OF THE CONSTITUTION STATES

*[The Congress shall have the Power] To establish an uniform rule of **Naturalization**, and uniform Laws on the subject of Bankruptcies throughout the United States.*

The Constitution gives Congress the express power to enact a uniform law of bankruptcy, which is the state or quality of financial ruin. A bankrupt person or business is insolvent, or unable to pay the debts owed to creditors. When the Framers wrote the Constitution in 1787, imprisonment and enslavement existed as punishment for persons who could not pay their debts. Even these harsh measures to enforce collection of debts were more humane than the remedy in ancient Rome, where creditors were permitted to dismember a debtor's body into equal parts.

The bankruptcy power has been one of the most flexible provisions in the Constitution. From 1800 on, changes have occurred in applying federal bankruptcy laws and the relief from debt they afforded. These changes are among the most prominent in the nation's legal history.

Early Nineteenth-Century Developments

The first Bankruptcy Act was passed in 1800. Its provisions were limited to merchants. All the bankrupt person's assets except the bedding and clothing of his or her family were to be used to pay creditors. If a large number of the creditors agreed, the bankrupt person could obtain a discharge from unpaid debts. This law was repealed in 1803, before its expiration date in 1805. One of the main reasons it failed was that creditors received little of their money because most bankrupt persons were put in prison.

The Bankruptcy Act of 1841 was the nation's second bankruptcy law. It was enacted as a result of a major economic depression that began in 1837. This law applied to both merchants and nonmerchants. It permitted a bankrupt debtor to keep more property exempt from the claims of creditors. The 1841 law also lowered the percentage of creditors needed to release a person from bankruptcy from two-thirds to a majority; but the majority needed to oppose rather than approve such a release. This law was repealed in 1843, probably because it had become easier for debtors to receive a discharge, a change which some creditors did not approve.

exempt free from a requirement that others are subject to

▶ The courts ordered the shutdown of United States Steel's Ohio works (1980), in spite of the workers' attempts to buy the plant and reorganize it.

Developments After the Civil War

The nation faced a major economic crisis after the Civil War. In part to cope with the crisis, Congress passed the Bankruptcy Act of 1867. This law extended debt relief to corporations as well as to individuals. Under it, a person could be discharged from bankruptcy with the agreement of fewer creditors than under earlier laws. The 1867 bankruptcy law was in effect for eleven years. It was repealed in 1878 because creditors were dissatisfied that they were receiving less money and bankrupt persons were receiving more benefits.

statute a law enacted by the legislative branch of government

During the periods when federal bankruptcy statutes did not exist, the states had their own insolvency, or bankruptcy, laws. But because the contract clause of the Constitution prevents a state from weakening a contract, the Supreme Court ruled, in *Macmillan* v. *McNeil* (1819), that a state law could not release a bankrupt person from any debt. As a result, such state laws had little effect. Then in *International Shoe Company* v. *Pinkus* (1928), the Court ruled that, under the supremacy clause of the Constitution, a bankruptcy law passed by Congress took precedence over all state bankruptcy laws.

Chapter 11 of the 1978 Federal Bankruptcy Act allows bankrupt companies to continue to operate and attempt to reorganize themselves while they are under the supervision of the court. A company typically files for Chapter 11 protection when it no longer can pay its current bills or its future expenses, including judgments against it in court.

Since 1987, Texaco, Macy's department stores, and such airlines as Continental and TWA have declared bankruptcy. In 1991, the Supreme Court ruled that individuals, too, could use this provision of the law. Individuals as a result can protect much more of their property against seizure by creditors than in the past. The extension of the bankruptcy code to individual debtors was a major reason that the number of personal bankruptcies reached nearly one million annually by the mid-1990s.

The nation's fourth bankruptcy law was the Bankruptcy Act of 1898. It allowed a person to be discharged from bankruptcy even without the approval of that person's creditors. Judicial officers, called referees in bankruptcy, assisted federal judges in administering this law. Over the years, these referees gradually assumed more of a judicial role in resolving disputes that arose during bankruptcy cases. In 1973 the title of bankruptcy judge replaced the title of referee.

During the 1930s, the Bankruptcy Act of 1898 was expanded in many ways. Debtors who were wage earners were permitted to pay creditors part of their income over three years. Railroads and other corporations declaring bankruptcy were allowed to reorganize, as were bankrupt local governments. Businesses were allowed to arrange to pay part or all of their debts over a long period. It was also possible to reorganize debts that were protected by real estate owned by an individual or by partners.

In 1978 a new Bankruptcy Code replaced the 1898 act, and it became effective in 1979. This law continued the broad-based provisions of the 1898 act for releasing the individual debtor from bankruptcy. It also combined those parts of the old law which allowed bankrupt businesses to reorganize. The code balanced the interests of debtors and creditors. Such bankruptcy cases were conducted in courts that are part of the federal judicial system, and bankruptcy judges presided over them. The Supreme Court, in its ruling in *Northern Pipeline Construction Company* v. *Marathon Pipeline Company* (1982), restricted the types of cases that the bankruptcy court hears, but the system continued to develop and work well. At the end of the twentieth century, it seemed that the 1978 Bankruptcy Code could even last another eighty years.

★ Fiscal and Monetary Powers
Joel B. Grossman and Mark V. Cushman

duty a tax on goods brought into the country

impost an imposed charge; a tax or duty

excise a tax that a government puts on the manufacture, sale, or use of a domestic product

debt an obligation to pay money or goods to another person

revenue income from investments, salary, or property; a government's sources of revenue include taxes and licenses

legislation the power and work of making laws

ARTICLE I, SECTION 8, CLAUSE 1, OF THE CONSTITUTION STATES

*[The Congress shall have the Power] To lay and collect Taxes, **Duties, Imposts** and **Excises**, to pay the **debts** and provide for the common Defense and general Welfare of the United States, but all Duties, Imposts and Excises shall be uniform throughout the United States.*

The fiscal and monetary powers of the federal government are the powers to tax and spend. Congress also is granted the power to borrow and coin money. In addition, Article I, Section 7, Clause 1, requires that all revenue bills must first be introduced in the House of Representatives. However, as with all legislation, the House and Senate must agree on identical wording of a revenue bill before it is presented to the president to sign into law.

The Power to Tax

fiscal relating to matters of finance

Articles of Confederation the first constitution of the thirteen original United States; in effect 1781–1789

levy impose or collect a tax

export merchandise sent to another place as part of commercial business

The decision to give Congress the broadest possible fiscal powers reflected the Framers' dissatisfaction with the Articles of Confederation. Under the Articles, the national government lacked the power to levy taxes or raise revenues directly. Instead, it had to depend on each state to contribute its share of government funds. Under the Constitution, by contrast, Congress has plenary, or complete, power to tax persons and property directly.

Although Congress's power to tax is quite broad, it has certain limits. Article I, Section 9, Clause 5, prohibits Congress from levying taxes or duties on exports. This clause was intended to satisfy the concerns of agricultural and slave states. Moreover, a distinction is made in other provisions between direct and indirect taxes. Direct taxes must be allotted among the states based on population, while indirect taxes must apply uniformly, or the same, to all persons, regardless of the state they live in. The Supreme Court has ruled that this uniformity requirement is geographic in nature and thus does not, for example, prohibit a progressive income tax that sets different tax rates for persons with different income levels.

The Framers were unclear in their use of the term "direct taxes." Its meaning was not finally defined until the Supreme Court held, in *Pollock* v. *Farmers' Loan & Trust Co.* (1895), that an income tax levied by Congress, and not allotted among the states, on all personal incomes above $4,000 was a direct tax, and therefore was unconstitutional. However, the

▶ Illustration of the budget process—an exhausted and ragged representative staggers away from a just-approved budget bill.

ratify to formally approve a document, thereby making it legal

enumerated powers the powers listed in a constitution; these powers also are sometimes called the *expressed* powers

The power to tax is also subject to other constitutional limitations, including the specific provisions of the Bill of Rights. In 1968, the Supreme Court ruled that the right against **self-incrimination** protects a person from being **prosecuted** for failing to register as a gambler as required by federal law and for failing to pay federal occupational and excise taxes. This tax required gamblers to keep careful records which the government could then use to force gamblers into confessing, in order to comply with this law, that they had violated the gambling laws of most states.

self-incrimination giving of testimony that will likely make a witness prosecutable

prosecute to begin and carry on a lawsuit; bring legal action against

ARTICLE I—The Tax and Spend Power

Sixteenth Amendment reversed this ruling. That amendment, which was ratified in 1913, gave Congress the power to tax incomes from all sources without allotting the tax.

The Power to Spend

Congress's power to spend, like its power to tax, also is very broad. The national legislature may appropriate money for any proper constitutional purpose. (This appropriation power includes spending to carry out the enumerated powers in Article I, Section 8, of the Constitution, such as establishing a post office, regulating currency, and providing for the national defense.) It also includes the less-defined power to spend for the general welfare. In one of its most important decisions, *McCulloch* v. *Maryland* (1819), the Supreme Court decided that the "necessary and proper" clause in Article I, Section 8, allowed Congress to create a national bank in order to carry out its enumerated power to regulate currency. As a result, a large part of all congressional spending is, in fact, for the purpose of carrying out its enumerated powers.

Nevertheless, most of the structure and growth of the welfare state since the New Deal of the 1930s has been funded under Congress's direct taxing and spending powers. Social Security, Medicare, and various education and welfare programs are funded in this way. The only limits are that such spending must be for the general welfare and that Congress may not spend funds that violate any limitation expressed in the Constitution. However, the Supreme Court has held that it is up to Congress to determine what the general welfare is.

The Supreme Court also has ruled that Congress may use its general spending power to promote the general welfare by attaching conditions for receiving federal funds. In *South Dakota* v. *Dole* (1987), the Court upheld an act of Congress that required states, in order to receive federal highway funds, to pass laws setting twenty-one as the minimum age for drinking alcoholic beverages. Thus, Congress's spending power may be used to regulate, even when, as in this case, it may not have been able to achieve the same result under the enumerated powers.

★ Postal Power
Jeffrey B. Morris

ARTICLE I, SECTION 8, CLAUSE 7, OF THE CONSTITUTION STATES

[The Congress shall have the Power] To establish post offices and post roads.

The postal clause of the Constitution authorizes Congress to establish a postal service, protect the mail, and ensure its efficient distribution. As the clause is now interpreted, Congress may use the postal power to subsidize, or provide funds for, industries that carry the mail, such as airlines, railroads, and shipping companies. It also may appropriate money to build and maintain roads for postal purposes.

The Early Years

The importance of the postal service in American history is sometimes forgotten. Before the invention of the telephone, automobiles, television, and other modern means of communication, the postal service played a key role in unifying the nation. Great Britain had been responsible for the postal service in the colonies before the American Revolution. Parliament in 1710 had created the position of deputy postmaster general for the colonies. Benjamin Franklin held that post from 1753 until 1774. Then, in 1775, the Second Continental Congress established an American postal system and made Franklin postmaster general. Under the **Articles of Confederation**, which went into effect in 1781, Congress was given the sole power to establish and regulate post offices that would send mail from one state to another and charge postage for this service.

When the national government under the Constitution began, some seventy-five post offices existed in the United States. The first Congress, in 1789, provided for a postmaster general. However, Congress did not establish the Post Office Department until 1795. The postmaster general became a member of the president's cabinet in 1829. The first United States postage stamps were authorized in 1846 and the first postcards in 1872. In 1970, however, Congress used the postal power to replace the Post Office Department with an independent governmental corporation, the United States Postal Service, in order to try to increase the efficiency of its operation.

The Postal Power in the Nineteenth Century

Even though the postal clause is quite short and does not seem hard to interpret, difficult questions have been raised about it. During the first half of the nineteenth century, a great debate was waged over whether the federal government had the power to construct public works in the states by spending federal funds directly to build roads, military highways, and canals. Those who favored this action argued that the postal clause authorized such spending. In 1817, the House of Representatives passed a resolution taking that position. However, Presidents Madison, Monroe, and Jackson took the other side, and money for such construction was not appropriated by Congress. Not until the 1870s was there agreement that the postal clause gave Congress the power to do more than decide which mail routes and post offices could carry the mail and ensure its safety. Not until 1876 did the Supreme Court hold that the federal government could buy land in order to build a post office.

During the nineteenth century, it became clear that state laws that limited or interfered with the mail were unconstitutional. In 1845, for example, the Supreme Court ruled that a state could not impose a tax on wagons carrying the mail. The Court in 1896 held that a state could not require an interstate mail train to make a seven-mile detour in order to stop at a particular station. State laws that indirectly affected postal service have been upheld, however. For example, a state may arrest a postal employee charged with murder even though he is engaged in carrying out his official duties.

Articles of Confederation the first constitution of the thirteen original United States; in effect 1781–1789

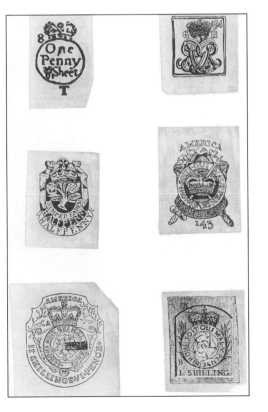

 Early American stamps.

abolitionist person favoring principles or measures fostering the end of slavery

seditious urging the disruption or overthrow of the government

🔺 The seal of the Society for the Suppression of Vice—the society's goal was to prohibit the handling and distribution through the mails of what they considered offensive materials.

censorship the official restriction of any expression believed to threaten the political, social, or moral order

obscenity material that is indecent, offensive, or disgusting, or to which the prevailing morality is strongly opposed

Anthony Comstock (1844–1915) crusaded against literature and art that he considered obscene. In 1873, he persuaded Congress to pass what became known as the "Comstock Law." This law made it a federal crime to mail "obscenity." Congress made Comstock a special agent of the post office with power to enforce this law. He brought to trial many people who were convicted and sent to jail. One story has it that in court during the trial of a woman who mailed pictures Comstock considered immoral, he told the judge, "Your Honor, this woman gave birth to a naked child."

The Impact of the First Amendment

Difficult questions have arisen when the exercise of the postal power has appeared to clash with other provisions of the Constitution. In 1829, some Congressmen attempted to force post offices to close on Sundays for a day of rest. The measure did not pass because many members of Congress believed that this violated the Constitution's separation of church and state. The hardest questions have involved the issue of whether either Congress or the post office itself may ban certain things from the mails. In the 1830s, abolitionists used the postal system to send tracts attacking slavery to Southerners. President Andrew Jackson urged passage of a law punishing the sending of such materials. Congress did not adopt this proposal because many members feared that doing so would give the national government too much power. Even so, Southern postmasters often destroyed such mail on their own authority.

By the last years of the nineteenth century, there was general agreement that since Congress had the power to decide what mail should be carried, it also could specify what mail could not be carried. Thus, lottery tickets, newspapers with ads for lotteries, obscene or indecent publications, and materials describing birth control and abortion were banned from the mail.

Controlling political speech. From time to time, Congress has used the postal power to censor political speech. During World War I, for example, the postmaster general prevented certain newspapers and magazines from using the cheaper rates of second-class mail because he claimed that they contained treasonable or seditious materials. In 1921, the Supreme Court, in its ruling in *Milwaukee Publishing Company* v. *Burleson*, upheld this practice. However, Justice Louis D. Brandeis, in a dissenting opinion, expressed concern that the postmaster general might become the "universal censor of publications." Justice Oliver Wendell Holmes, in another dissenting opinion in *Burleson*, argued that "the use of the mails is almost as much a part of free speech as the right to use our tongues."

During the first year of World War II, seventy newspapers and periodicals were barred from the mails. However, in its 1965 ruling in *Lamont* v. *Postmaster General,* the Supreme Court struck down a law that permitted the Post Office Department not to forward mail that it said was Communist propaganda. The law also required that the persons to whom this mail was addressed must then request that it be forwarded to them. The *Lamont* decision was the first time the Supreme Court ever held a federal law unconstitutional on free speech grounds.

Censorship. The postal power also has been used by Congress to try to ban books and magazines from the mails on the grounds of obscenity or indecency. In the late 1800s and the early 1900s, the Post Office Department prohibited the mailing of Boccaccio's *Decameron* and some of the works of Leo Tolstoy. Indeed, the department actually burned a copy of James Joyce's *Ulysses.* However, changes in public attitudes about censorship and sexually oriented speech led to limits on such use of the postal power. During World War II, the postmaster general sought to take away second-class mailing privileges from *Esquire* magazine. That official

FIRST AMENDMENT—
The First Amendment

claimed that the publication was vulgar, in poor taste, and was not "disseminating information of a public character." In a 1945 decision, the Supreme Court ruled that this official did not have the power of censorship.

Although it was much harder in the late 1990s to prevent something being sent through the mail on the ground that it was obscene, the Supreme Court has ruled that some publications, though legal if possessed by individuals in private, can be barred from the mails. The high Court also has upheld a law requiring the Postal Service to keep a list of people who inform it that they do not want to receive sexually oriented mail. Moreover, in the 1990s, the Court ruled that laws aimed at preventing the mailing of pornographic material containing photographs of children are constitutional. Yet, at the same time, the Court has made convicting persons charged with violating such laws more difficult.

Copyright and Patents
Neil Weinstock Netanel

copyright law laws that protect the rights of authors

patent law laws that protect the rights of inventors

ARTICLE 1, SECTION 8, CLAUSE 8, OF THE CONSTITUTION STATES

[The Congress shall have the Power] To promote the Progress of Science and the useful Arts, by securing for limited Times to Authors and Inventors the exclusive Right to their respective Writings and Discoveries.

Copyright law gives authors a set of exclusive rights to the writings they produce. Under copyright law, no one may copy a book, play a song over the radio or on television, or make a film based on a novel unless the author or songwriter grants permission to do so. **Patent law** gives inventors the right to prevent anyone from making, using, selling, or importing their patented inventions.

The Constitution gives Congress the power to enact many types of laws. But only the copyright and patent clause sets forth the Framers' specific goal for Congress's passing such laws—to "promote the progress of science and the useful arts." At the time the Constitution was written, the word "science" meant knowledge of all kinds, and "useful arts" referred to practical know-how.

The Framers' View

The Framers believed that copyright and patent law would provide an incentive for authors to create books that advance knowledge and for inventors to share technological know-how and to devise new tools, machines, and products that would better people's lives. The law would provide this incentive by giving authors and inventors an opportunity to market their creative products free from competitors who would otherwise take the fruits of authors' and inventors' intellectual labor without paying for it. By enabling authors and inventors to earn income from their writings and discoveries, copyright and patent law would benefit not only them, but all of society. As James Madison wrote in support of including the copyright and patent clause in the Constitution, protecting

A product label with an illustrated portrait of Thomas Alva Edison surrounded by objects of his invention.

the rights of authors and inventors is an instance in which "the public good fully coincides . . . with claims of individuals."

Origins of Copyright and Patent Law

The idea of giving such an incentive to authors and inventors did not begin with the Framers. American copyright and patent laws owe their origins to English statutes enacted long before the Constitution was adopted. The first modern patent law was the English Statute of Monopolies of 1624, and the first modern copyright law was the English Statute of [Queen] Anne of 1710.

No general copyright or patent laws were enacted in the American colonies, but colonial authorities sometimes granted individual patents. In addition, authors' rights to prevent unauthorized publication of their manuscripts were protected under judge-made common law. In 1783, the Continental Congress passed a resolution recommending that the states pass copyright laws and, by the time of the Constitutional Convention in 1787, twelve of the thirteen states had done so. Nevertheless, the Framers recognized the need for a federal copyright law and patent law. Otherwise authors and inventors throughout the country would have to apply to thirteen different states.

It did not take long for Congress to exercise its power under the copyright and patent clause to protect the rights of authors and inventors. In 1790, it passed the first federal copyright and patent laws. The first copyright statute, called "An Act for the Encouragement of Learning," gave authors an exclusive right to make copies of their maps, navigational charts, and books for a once-renewable term of fourteen years. The first patent statute, called "An Act to Promote the Progress of Useful Arts," gave inventors an exclusive right to produce and sell their inventions for a period of fourteen years.

Contemporary Copyright and Patent Laws

Modern copyright and patent laws are intended to serve the same purposes as the nation's first laws. Only the details are different. One difference is that the terms of protection cover considerably longer periods. A patent remains in force for twenty years from the time it was applied for, while a copyright lasts for the lifetime of the author plus fifty years.

Modern copyrights protect not only writings but also visual art, plays, photographs, films, television shows, recordings, architecture, and computer programs. Authors enjoy the exclusive right not just to make copies of their works, but also to publicly perform and display them, as well as to adapt them for new and different media.

Modern patents also cover new rights and types of inventions, yet it was in many ways more difficult to obtain a patent at the end of the twentieth century than it was in 1790. In the early decades of patent law, patents were issued almost automatically. Since the middle of the nineteenth century, inventors have been able to get a patent only if they can convince a trained examiner that their invention is useful, new, and different enough.

statute a law enacted by the legislative branch of government

common law the system of judge-made law that began in England and is based on court decisions and custom rather than on statutes passed by legislatures

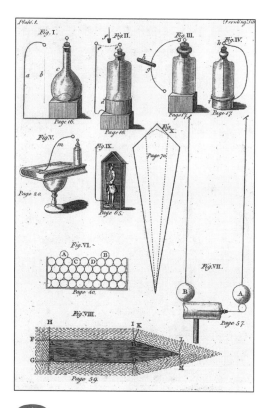

Benjamin Franklin (1706–1790) was a statesman, a philosopher, and a scientist. This is his electrical apparatus as it appeared in his *Experiments and Observations on Electricity*, a book he wrote and published on his own printing press.

Limitations on Rights

In carrying out the constitutional goal of promoting knowledge, modern copyright and patent law limits the rights of authors and inventors in important ways. When their term of protection comes to an end, creative products enter the public domain. Moreover, under certain conditions, anyone may use protected products without permission from the copyright or patent holder, even during the term of protection.

The doctrine of "fair use" also limits copyright law protection. Under this doctrine, anyone may copy parts of a copyrighted work for purposes that benefit society, such as for news reporting, parody, and criticism, as long as such copying does not interfere too much with the market for that work. In the same way, patent law recognizes an exception for experimental use. This allows for the construction and use of a patented invention for noncommercial basic research. Whether the limits on authors' and inventors' rights should be increased or reduced in order to serve the public interest best is one of the most difficult questions in copyright and patent law.

Supreme Court Rulings

Another controversial question is the extent to which the Constitution limits Congress's power to grant rights over intellectual products. The Supreme Court has ruled that the copyright and patent clause does not empower Congress to grant rights to noncreative and nonoriginal products, such as the alphabetical listing of names in the white pages of a telephone directory. It is quite possible, however, that Congress could grant such rights under its power to regulate commerce. The First Amendment's protection of free speech might make unenforceable too broad an application of copyright owners' rights.

As the Supreme Court has stressed in its rulings, copyright generally serves as "the engine of free expression" by providing authors with an important incentive to contribute to society's knowledge and to public debate on political, social, and cultural issues. Yet if copyright owners could prevent others from drawing upon the ideas contained in their books, films, and other works, or if Congress were to end or greatly restrict the fair use doctrine, it would chill the free exchange of ideas and might well conflict with the First Amendment.

public domain the condition of being unprotected by copyright or patent and open to use by anyone

Thomas Alva Edison patented over one thousand inventions, more than any other person. Among them were the microphone (1877), the phonograph, which some people called a "speaking machine," the phonograph record, the stock ticker, the stencil, and the incandescent light bulb. In 1881–1882 in New York City, Edison installed the world's first central electric power plant. This led to making electricity widely available. In 1883 he pioneered the radio tube, using a method for passing electricity from a filament to a plate of metal inside an incandescent light globe. Edison also developed the first motion picture camera and projector, and was working on talking movies when a fire destroyed the part of his laboratory containing this work.

★ Offenses Against the Law of Nations
Roger K. Newman

felony a crime usually punished by death or a lengthy prison sentence

law of nations a term that means international law; a set of rules that the nations of the world have agreed to follow in their relations with one another

ARTICLE I, SECTION 8, CLAUSE 10, STATES

[The Congress shall have the Power] To define and punish Piracies and Felonies committed on the high Seas, and Offenses against the Law of Nations.

The United States became subject to the law of nations when it became an independent country in 1781. Although the Continental Congress had accepted the law of nations during the American Revolution, the Articles of Confederation, the nation's first constitution, made no provision for dealing with offenses against the law of nations.

But the Articles did give Congress power to set up courts to try acts of piracy and felonies committed on the high seas. The first draft of the Constitution expanded this power, giving Congress authority "to declare the law and punishment of piracies and felonies committed on the high seas, and the punishment of counterfeiting the coin of the United States, and of offenses against the law of nations."

Congress to define the clause. Some Framers of the Constitution questioned whether the terms "felonies" and "law of nations" were precise enough to be clearly understood. After debating this question, the delegates agreed that those terms were indeed too vague, and they authorized Congress to give meaning to all the words in the clause.

Over the years, Congress passed several laws to define the law of nations clause. In 1820, the Supreme Court upheld an act of Congress that punished "the crime of piracy, as the law of nations" defined piracy. That act referred to international law, and the Court ruled that the meaning of this term was clear enough. International law has always been based more on nations' conduct and general practices than on precise regulations. The Supreme Court has almost always accepted these general practices in deciding cases that involved the law of nations clause. In 1887 the Court upheld Congress's power to declare it a crime to forge copies of another nation's government bonds and notes. The justices reasoned that each country has a duty to prevent wrongful acts within its borders against another country with which it is at peace.

Offenses against the law of war. In 1942, the Supreme Court ruled that a military trial for offenses against the law of war was constitutional. Four years later, in *re Yamashita* (1946), the justices held that the law of nations clause gave Congress the power to set up a military commission to serve as a tribunal for "the trial and punishment of offenses against the law of war." Yet the Court has seldom cited this constitutional provision.

The law of nations clause is the only part of the Constitution that grants power to punish offenses committed outside the borders of the

---

In *The Federalist*, No. 42, James Madison wrote that the Articles of Confederation "contain no provision for the case of offenses against the law of nations; and consequently leave it in the power of any indiscreet member [a state] to embroil the **Confederacy** with foreign nations. The provision of the [proposed Constitution] on the subject of piracies and felonies extends no further than to the establishment of courts for the trial of these offenses. The definition of piracies might . . . be left to the law of nations; though a legislative definition of them is found in most municipal codes."

Confederacy the single unit formed by persons, states, or nations united by a common political purpose; here, the thirteen original United States

▼ A newspaper account of the slaves' revolt aboard the *Amistad* in July of 1839.

Death of Capt. Ferrer, the Captain of the Amistad, July, 1839.

Don Jose Ruiz and Don Pedro Montez, of the Island of Cuba, having purchased fifty-three slaves at Havana, recently imported from Africa, put them on board the Amistad, Capt. Ferrer, in order to transport them to Principe, another port on the Island of Cuba. After being out from Havana about four days, the African captives on board, in order to obtain their freedom, and return to Africa, armed themselves with cane knives, and rose upon the Captain and crew of the vessel. Capt. Ferrer and the cook of the vessel were killed; two of the crew escaped; Ruiz and Montez were made prisoners.

United States. The Supreme Court has ruled that the federal government's power over admiralty and maritime cases covers offenses committed on ships outside the United States but not on the high seas, which begin ten miles off the nation's coast. But the Court has also ruled that an offense committed on a ship anchored in another nation's waters is considered to be like one on the high seas.

International law has traditionally dealt with governments rather than individuals. But the atrocities and terrible mass crimes committed by totalitarian governments during the twentieth century have led to an increasing emphasis on the role of international law in protecting individuals. This expanded role may give the law of nations clause a new and unexpected importance.

The War Power
Louis Fisher

letters of marque and reprisal documents issued by Congress (no longer used) that allowed private citizens to arm a ship and help American military forces; they helped by capturing enemy merchant ships and cargo, and by taking prisoners on land or at sea

defensive protecting against aggression or attack

offensive marked by aggressive action that is initiated rather than defensive

vest to grant with particular authority, property, and rights

ARTICLE I, SECTION 8, CLAUSE 11, OF THE CONSTITUTION STATES

*[The Congress shall have the Power] To declare War, grant **Letters of Marque and Reprisal**, and make Rules concerning Captures on Land and Water . . .*

The Constitution divides the war power between Congress and the president. The Framers gave Congress the primary authority for initiating military action against other nations. The president, as commander in chief, would lead troops and be responsible for taking emergency defensive action. For most of the nineteenth and the first half of the twentieth century, this distribution of power was largely followed. However, beginning in 1950 with the Korean War, presidents have grown accustomed to using the war power at their own initiative for offensive military actions, without first seeking approval and authority from Congress.

Framing the War Power

Article I, Section 8, of the Constitution grants Congress a number of significant powers related to military activity. It gives Congress the power to "declare war, grant letters of marque and reprisal, and make rules concerning captures on land and water." The Framers knew that in Great Britain the power to declare war was vested in the king. In keeping with Republican government, the Framers gave this power to Congress.

The wording of the clause. At the Constitutional Convention, the Framers debated the phrase to "declare war." In an early draft, they authorized Congress to "make" war. Charles Pinckney, one of the delegates, objected, saying that Congress should not be given the power to make war, because legislative procedures "were too slow" to be effective in an emergency. The country would be at risk if Congress failed to act promptly, and Pinckney and other delegates expected Congress to meet only once each year. James Madison and Elbridge Gerry suggested using the word "declare" instead of "make," leaving the president "the power to repel sudden attacks." This new wording was approved.

A defensive power. The Framers expected the president to take certain defensive actions when the country was threatened. The president was given power to repel sudden attacks in an emergency, when Congress was not in session or was unable to respond quickly. Some delegates stressed the limited nature of the president's war power. As Roger Sherman explained, the president "should be able to repel and not to commence war." Elbridge Gerry agreed, saying that he "never expected to hear in a republic a motion to empower the executive alone to declare war." George Mason spoke against "giving the power of war to the executive" because that officer could not be safely "trusted with it," and Mason was "for clogging rather than facilitating war."

At the Pennsylvania convention called to ratify the Constitution, James Wilson expressed his satisfaction that the Constitution's system of checks and balances "will not hurry us into war; it is calculated to guard against it. It will not be in the power of a single man, or a single body of men, to involve us in such distress; for the important power of declaring war is vested in the legislature at large."

Congress to retain ultimate war power. Madison strongly opposed any action by a president to initiate a war. He argued that this power should be reserved solely for Congress. "Those who are to conduct a war cannot in the nature of things, be proper or safe judges, whether a war ought to be commenced, continued, or concluded," Madison declared. "They are barred from the latter function by a great principle in free government, analogous to that which separates the sword from the purse, or the power of executing from the power of enacting laws."

Other Constitutional Provisions Affecting the War Power

Other provisions in Article I, Section 8, add to the powers of Congress over the military. Congress is given the power to "raise and support armies, but no **appropriation** of money to that use shall be for a longer term than two years." Congress has the power to "provide and maintain a navy," the power to "make rules for the government and regulation of the land and naval forces," and the power to provide for "calling forth the **militia** to execute the laws of the Union, suppress insurrections and repel invasions." Congress also has the power to provide for "organizing, arming, and disciplining, the militia, and for governing such part of them as may be employed in the service of the United States, reserving to the states respectively, the appointment of the officers, and the authority of training the militia according to the discipline prescribed by Congress."

The power of the purse is a vital **prerogative** of Congress to control military actions. Under Article I, Section 9, Clause 7, "No money shall be drawn from the treasury, but in consequence of appropriations made by law." Congress alone has the power to appropriate funds and to decide precisely how they will be spent. After reviewing the draft constitution,

ratify to formally approve a document, thereby making it legal

appropriation the setting aside for or assigning to a particular purpose or use

militia a part-time army made up of ordinary citizens

prerogative having to do with a special right or privilege particular to an office

84

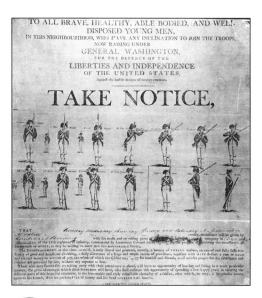

A 1798 recruiting poster summons young men to an army under the command of George Washington. The former president was commissioned to command an army being readied for a possible war against France.

Thomas Jefferson praised the delegates' decision to transfer the war power "from the executive to the legislative body, from those who are to spend to those who are to pay." At the Constitutional Convention, George Mason warned that the "purse and the sword ought never to get into the same hands—whether legislative or executive."

The Constitution's Pattern

The Constitution's design is clear and consistent. The Framers rejected the British theory that linked the power of war and peace with the monarchy. Charles Pinckney, for example, supported a vigorous executive, but he "was afraid the executive powers . . . might extend to peace & war &c. which would render the executive a monarchy, of the worst kind, to wit an elective one." John Rutledge, too, favored a single executive, though he "was not for giving him the power of war and peace." James Wilson, who also wanted a single executive, did not consider "the Prerogatives of the British Monarch as a proper guide in defining the Executive powers. Some of these prerogatives were of a Legislative nature. Among others that of war & peace, &c."

Congress to control the military. In *The Federalist*, No. 69, Alexander Hamilton explained the difference between the American president and the British king. The power of the monarch "extends to the declaring of war and to the raising and regulating of fleets and armies." Unlike the British king, the president "will have only the occasional command of such part of the militia of the nation as by legislative provision may be called into the actual service of the Union."

The Framers widely supported placing the power of war in legislators rather than in the president. Madison argued that the Constitution "supposes, what the history of all governments demonstrates, that the executive is the branch of power most interested in war, and most prone to it. It has accordingly with studied care, vested the question of war in the legislature."

Congress to authorize hostilities. In addition to declared wars, Congress may pass legislation to authorize military action against other nations. Congress in 1798 enacted a number of **statutes** authorizing war against France. Because there was no formal declaration of war, this conflict with France was called a "quasi-war." This meant that the lawmakers knew that Congress had authorized war, even though war was never actually declared. As Congressman Edward Livingston remarked during the debate on the 1798 act, he considered the United States "now in a state of war, and let no man flatter himself that the vote which has been given is not a declaration of war."

Supreme Court rulings. The quasi-war with France led to several important judicial decisions. In two rulings, the Supreme Court recognized that Congress could authorize hostilities either by a formal declaration of war or by statutes that authorize an undeclared war. In the first decision, in *Bas* v. *Tingy* (1800), the Court stated that military conflicts could be "limited," "partial," and "imperfect," without requiring Congress

statute a law enacted by the legislative branch of government

85

to make a formal declaration of war. In the second case, *Talbot* v. *Seeman* (1801), Chief Justice John Marshall wrote for the Court: "The whole powers of war being, by the Constitution of the United States, vested in Congress, the acts of that body can alone be resorted to as our guides in this inquiry."

Presidential Power Expands

Congress has declared war on five occasions: the War of 1812 against England, the Mexican War in 1846, the Spanish-American War in 1898, World War I in 1917, and World War II in 1941. Presidents have used military force in many lesser conflicts, often without authorization from Congress. These actions were often defended by presidents as necessary to protect American lives and property.

The major expansion of the presidential war power occurred after World War II. In 1950, President Harry Truman ordered American air and sea forces to assist South Korea when North Korea invaded it. Although he called the war a United Nations (UN) "police action," that organization exercised no authority over the conduct of the war. It was a war fought by the United States, with only token support from a few other nations. President Truman never sought or obtained authority from Congress for sending American forces to Korea.

Another presidential initiative came in 1964, when President Lyndon Johnson convinced Congress to pass the Gulf of Tonkin Resolution that approved and supported "the determination of the President, as Commander in Chief, to take all necessary measures to repel any armed attack against the forces of the United States and to prevent further aggression." Military operations in Vietnam continued and expanded under President Richard Nixon, reaching into Laos and Cambodia.

"Without the authority of Congress, the President cannot fire a hostile gun in any case except to repel the attacks of the enemy."

—James Buchanan (1791–1868), Fifteenth president of the United States

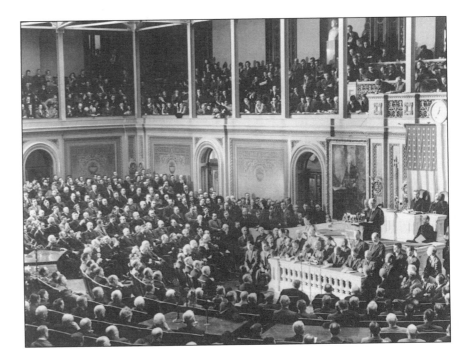

On December 8, 1941, President Franklin D. Roosevelt asked Congress to declare war on Japan in answer to the surprise attack on Pearl Harbor.

The War Powers Resolution of 1973

From 1970 to 1973, Congress drafted legislation to curb the president's power to initiate a war. As enacted in 1973, the War Powers Resolution calls for the "collective judgment" of both Congress and the president before American troops may be sent into combat. But other sections of the resolution expanded executive power by permitting the president to use military force for up to ninety days without first getting congressional consent—a scope for presidential powers greater than the Framers ever imagined.

Experience with the War Powers Resolution in its first two decades suggested that presidents would still respond to short-term emergencies on their own but seek Congress's approval for major commitments of troops. Thus, President Gerald Ford acted without congressional authority in Cambodia in capturing the ship *Mayaguez* in 1975, as did President Ronald Reagan in taking military action in Grenada in 1983 and against Libya in 1986. But long-term military engagements, including Lebanon in 1983 and Iraq during the Persian Gulf war in 1991, required explicit congressional approval.

Weakness of the War Powers Resolution

This division of power began to break down during the administration of President Bill Clinton. He was prepared to invade Haiti in 1994 without first obtaining authority from Congress, though this action became unnecessary. Clinton also conducted American air strikes in Bosnia and sent twenty thousand troops there in 1995, again without seeking legislative authority. The legality of these operations was complicated by Clinton's claim that he could invade Haiti partly on the basis of a UN Security Council resolution, while relying on a mix of UN and NATO (North Atlantic Treaty Organization) authority for his actions in Bosnia. The language and history of the UN Charter and NATO do not support such broad definitions of presidential power.

Four times during the Reagan administration (1981–1989), members of Congress went to court to challenge the President's war initiatives. They asked federal judges to rule unconstitutional and illegal President Reagan's military actions in El Salvador, Nicaragua, Grenada, and the Persian Gulf. Each time the result was the same. In *Crockett* v. *Reagan*, *Sanchez-Espinoza* v. *Reagan*, *Conyers* v. *Reagan*, and *Lowry* v. *Reagan*, the federal courts told Congress: If you fail to challenge the president, don't come to us. They made it clear that Congress must be willing to use its own institutional powers to check the president.

In 1990, President George Bush claimed that he could take offensive military actions against Iraq without obtaining congressional authority. As Truman had done in Korea, Bush relied in part on a UN Security Council resolution. Members of Congress again went to court to challenge this interpretation of executive power. In *Dellums* v. *Bush*, a federal judge rejected the sweeping interpretation of presidential power advanced by the Department of Justice. But since Bush had not yet used military force against Iraq, the judge rejected the case on the grounds that a court

see also

ARTICLE II—Commander-in-Chief;
The Executive Branch;
National Security and the Presidency;
Presidential Emergency Powers

should not decide a case before it is necessary to do so. A few weeks later, Bush sought, and obtained, authority from Congress to act.

The lesson about the war power from these statutes and court cases is clear. If members of Congress want to protect their prerogatives and maintain the division of power designed by the Framers, they must be willing to challenge the president through the institutional powers available to Congress. These include the power of the purse and the passing of laws with language that specifically prohibits the president from taking certain actions.

★ Armed Forces
Robert J. Cottrol

appropriation the setting aside for or assigning to a particular purpose or use

ARTICLE I, SECTION 8, CLAUSE 11, OF THE CONSTITUTION STATES

*[The Congress shall have the Power] To raise and support armies, but no **Appropriation** of Money to that Use shall be for a longer Term than two Years;*

To provide and maintain a Navy;

To make Rules for the Government and Regulation of the land and naval forces.

The Constitution's relationship to the modern American armed forces presents something of a paradox. At the end of the twentieth century, the United States was unquestionably the world's strongest military power. Yet the Constitution is the product of men who deeply distrusted military power and who included provisions in the Constitution to clearly limit that power.

The Framers and the Armed Forces

The Framers of the Constitution were worried about having a standing or professional army. This mistrust came from their experience before the Revolution, when British troops were seen as an occupying army that endangered the freedom of the people.

Limit the power of the armed forces. Several provisions of the Constitution and the Bill of Rights were designed to prevent a standing army from becoming a threat to liberty. Congress is not given the power to maintain an army but to raise armies. Congress can appropriate money for only two years to raise an army. The Constitution does allow Congress to maintain a navy on a permanent basis. The Framers believed that an army could be turned against the people to support or establish tyranny while a navy was less likely to be misused.

The militia. Other constitutional provisions designed to prevent a possible military threat to individual rights deal with civilian control of the military. These provisions make the president the commander in chief of the armed forces and give Congress power to make laws governing the military. Other constitutional provisions relating to the militia were also designed to limit the power of a standing army. The idea was that a large

militia a part-time army made up of ordinary citizens

The Constitution gives Congress the power to declare war. The War Powers Resolution of 1973 requires that the president consult with Congress before sending the armed forces into combat.

Conscription was first introduced in the United States during the Civil War. All able-bodied men were required to serve in the armed forces, but a law passed by Congress in 1863 enabled any man to be exempted from the Union Army if he hired a substitute soldier for $300. The Supreme Court upheld the Selective Service Act of 1917, which required all men between the ages of 21 and 30 to register. By the end of World War I, 2.8 million men had been inducted. Peacetime conscription began in 1940. Ten million men were inducted between 1940 and 1947, two years after World War II ended. The draft supplied the military during the Korean and Vietnam hostilities. In 1973 an all-volunteer system replaced it. A pre-draft registration system for men between the ages of 18 and 26 was introduced in 1980.

civilian militia would provide a balance of forces and make it impossible for the army to seize power.

While the Framers' main concern in the late eighteenth century was to limit the size and power of the army to ensure that it would not become a threat to democratic government, the military concerns of Americans in the twentieth century have been quite different. Strong military threats posed by anti-democratic nations such as imperial Germany, Fascist Italy, Nazi Germany, empire-building Japan, and the Soviet Union forced Americans to address the issues of how to raise and maintain strong armed forces while observing what the Constitution says about how such forces are to be governed.

Supreme Court Rulings

The Supreme Court has been called on to settle disputes concerning the power of Congress to raise, support, and make laws governing the military, as well as the power of the president to act as commander in chief of the armed forces. Traditionally, the Court has taken the view that Congress and the president should be given considerable freedom of action in carrying out their respective powers because the Constitution gives the executive and legislative branches the authority to conduct foreign policy, make war, and control the armed forces.

The draft. A number of Supreme Court cases have concerned the issue of the draft. Draft laws passed by Congress have required that Americans must serve in the armed forces. The Court has supported Congress's power to establish a military draft in peacetime as well as in time of war as part of that body's authority to raise armies. The Court has ruled that conscription is not a violation of the Thirteenth Amendment's prohibition of involuntary servitude.

draft the act of selecting for compulsory military service

conscription enforced enrollment, particularly for military service

see also

ARTICLE I—Militia; The War Power;
ARTICLE II—Commander-in-Chief

The National Guard. The status of the National Guard has also come before the Supreme Court. Although the Guard is part of the militia in various states, it is also a permanent reserve of the armed forces. In *Perpich* v. *Department of Defense* (1990), the Court ruled that the president may send the National Guard overseas even over the objections of state governors.

The War Powers Resolution. It is unclear which branch of government prevails when the president and Congress disagree over sending American troops overseas. The Constitution gives Congress the power to declare war, but the president as commander in chief may send the armed forces into war zones or areas likely to become war zones.

In 1973, Congress passed the War Powers Resolution, which requires that the president consult with Congress before sending the armed forces into combat. The resolution also set a limit of sixty days on the dispatch of troops without the consent of Congress into areas where hostilities exist. Although some legal scholars believe that this resolution unconstitutionally limits the president's authority as commander in chief, the Supreme Court has yet to hear a case on the issue.

★ Militia
Robert J. Cottrol

militia a part-time army made up of ordinary citizens

ARTICLE I, SECTION 8, CLAUSE 14, OF THE CONSTITUTION STATES

*[The Congress shall have the Power] To provide for calling forth the **Militia** to execute the Laws of the Union, suppress Insurrections and repel Invasions;*

To provide for organizing, arming, and disciplining the Militia, and for governing such Part of them as may be employed in the Service of the United States, reserving to the States respectively, the Appointment of the Officers, and the Authority of training the Militia according to the discipline prescribed by Congress.

In the late eighteenth century, Americans feared a regular army as a threat to liberty. They preferred a militia instead, which would be controlled by the individual states except in times of national emergency.

The Militia in the Constitution

This prevailing view led the Framers to write several provisions in the Constitution to govern the militia. Article I, Section 8, Clause 14, gives Congress the authority to call forth the militia in order to execute the laws as well as to fight insurrections and invasions. It also grants Congress the power to organize, arm, and discipline the militia; and it makes the president the commander in chief of the militia when it is called into federal service. In addition, the Second Amendment to the Constitution expresses the view that "a well regulated militia is necessary to the security of a free state [nation]."

 The Massachusetts militia was sent to guard the mills in Lawrence during the 1912 labor strike.

see also

ARTICLE I—Armed Forces;
ARTICLE II—Commander-in-Chief

national guard the organized militia in each state or territory; at the same time a reserve of the United States army or air force

The National Guard has frequently been used during the twentieth century to restore peace and order. Massachusetts governor Calvin Coolidge (who later became president) used it to end a Boston police strike in 1919. President John F. Kennedy twice federalized Alabama's National Guard in 1963. This enabled two African-American students to enroll at the University of Alabama and permitted the desegregation of public schools in three Alabama cities. Governors called upon it in the Newark and Detroit riots in 1967. In 1974 a Massachusetts federal judge called out the National Guard to prevent racial warfare when violence broke out after he had ordered busing of public school students.

Late-eighteenth-century Americans believed that the militia should be composed of civilians from the population at large. The first militia act passed by Congress in 1792 made all free white men between the ages of 18 and 45 members of the militia of their states.

During the nineteenth century, the original idea of a population-based militia proved unworkable militarily. It was difficult to get the population as a whole to take militia drills seriously. Although state governors often found the militia useful during local emergencies, state militias were generally not effective when called into federal military service during war.

The National Guard

To remedy this weakness, Congress in the twentieth century passed legislation designed to increase the military efficiency of the militia. These measures divided the militia into the unorganized militia, which includes all males between ages 18 and 45, and the National Guard.

The National Guard is under the command of the governor of the state or territory, and the governor may use it in state emergencies. As a reserve of the United States army or air force, the president may call out the National Guard along with other military forces to protect the national security. National Guard units have fought in all of the nation's wars, and at the close of the twentieth century, they were serving in peacekeeping operations in Bosnia.

Because the National Guard is a reserve of the regular armed forces, as well as the organized state militia, the president is the commander in chief of the National Guard in peacetime and in times of national emergency. In *Perpich* v. *Department of Defense* (1990), the Supreme Court ruled that the president has the power to send National Guard units overseas in peacetime even over the objection of state governors.

Some states maintain militia units that are not part of the National Guard that would be available to state authorities when the Guard is deployed overseas. Governors also retain the authority to call upon the population at large during emergencies.

Governing the District of Columbia

Jeffrey B. Morris

legislation the power and work of making laws

*[The Congress shall have the Power] To exercise exclusive **legislation** in all cases whatsoever, over such district (not exceeding ten miles square) as may, by cession of particular States, and the acceptance of Congress, become the seat of the Government of the United States, and to exercise like authority over all places, purchased by the consent of the legislature of the State in which the same shall be, for the erection of forts, magazines, arsenals, dockyards, and other needful buildings.*

This provision of the Constitution gives Congress complete authority over the nation's capital. In 1790, Congress, using this power, decided that the capital would be built on land given to the United States by the states of Maryland and Virginia. Congress also gave the residents of Washington, D.C., a form of partial self-government in the late twentieth century, though Congress can change that form if it wishes. The people who live in Washington, D.C., elect a mayor and a city council as well as a non-voting delegate to Congress. However, this

An 1892 Currier & Ives map of Washington, D.C.

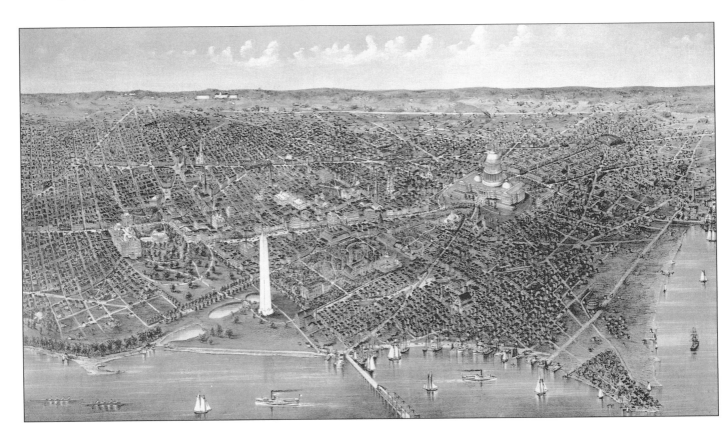

revenue income from investments, salary, or property; a government's sources of revenue include taxes and licenses

Articles of Confederation the first constitution of the thirteen original United States; in effect 1781–1789

government has only limited power to raise **revenue**. Except for the right to complete self-government, the people of Washington, D.C., have all the same constitutional rights as other Americans.

Choosing a Site

The security of the capital of the United States was a serious concern to the Framers of the Constitution. They were mindful that the Continental Congress had been forced to move from place to place by the tide of battle during the American Revolution. In June of 1783, Congress even had to flee from Philadelphia, then the capital, when angry Continental soldiers seeking their pay threatened its members. Nor did the officials of that city or the state come to Congress's assistance. In addition, the Framers had another concern. They also worried that if they chose some existing large city as the capital, the national government might come under the influence of its local merchants and bankers.

The last capital of the United States government under the **Articles of Confederation** was New York City, and it became the temporary capital until Congress decided on a plan. Both the North and the South wanted the capital, and a number of cities in each section hoped to be chosen as the site. In the end, a political deal determined the location of the capital. Several southern members of Congress agreed to support Secretary of the Treasury Alexander Hamilton's financial program in exchange for the votes of northern Congressmen to locate the capital on the Potomac River south of the Mason-Dixon line. Philadelphia was given the consolation prize: The government of the United States was to be in that city for ten years until the new capital was built.

A sign pleading for statehood for Washington, D.C.

Washington, D.C., the New Capital

As Congress provided, the exact location of the capital was chosen by President George Washington. He chose a site not far from his estate, Mt. Vernon. Maryland and Virginia gave the land for the ten-mile-square district. (Virginia's land was not needed and was returned to it in 1846.) The site Washington chose, which became known as the District of Columbia, was largely unsettled farmland and forest. It did, however, include the two small port cities of Alexandria and Georgetown along the Potomac River.

The United States government moved from Philadelphia to the District of Columbia in 1800. The White House was still unfinished when President John Adams, its first occupant, moved in. One week before Thomas Jefferson was inaugurated as president on March 4, 1801, Congress established a court system for the new District. Originally, this system set five separate governments in the District of Columbia—those of the cities of Washington, Georgetown, and Alexandria and two sparsely populated counties on the Virginia and Maryland sides of the Potomac.

Changes in Government in the District

Congress has such complete power over the District of Columbia that it may provide it with whatever officials and form of government Congress wants. At first, Congress specified that the mayor of the city of Washington be appointed by the president. From 1820 until 1871, the city was self-governing with an elected mayor. In 1871, the District of Columbia was unified. A single government was established, headed by a governor and a council appointed by the president, as well as an elected council. However, as a result of scandals connected with the rapid development of the District, Congress again changed its form of government. Three commissioners appointed by the president governed Washington, D.C., from 1878 to 1976.

After the Second World War, pressures for self-government in Washington intensified. As the African-American population of the city increased, there was growing dissatisfaction with a system in which southern congressmen controlled the policy-making committees in Washington. Many residents believed those congressmen were deeply prejudiced against African Americans.

In 1961, the Twenty-third Amendment to the Constitution was adopted, giving the residents of Washington, D.C., the right to vote in presidential elections. In 1967, President Lyndon Johnson reorganized the government of the District of Columbia, appointing a city council and mayor-commissioner, a position for which he chose an African American. That same year, Congress gave the people of Washington the right to elect their school board. In 1971, Congress provided that residents could elect a non-voting delegate to Congress. Then two years later, Congress passed the District of Columbia Self-Government Act. This act gave residents the right to elect a mayor and city council, although these officials' authority was limited. Congress itself retains final authority, as provided in the Constitution.

TWENTY-THIRD AMENDMENT

Some Washington, D.C., residents seek an arrangement whereby the United States would retain only the major governmental buildings. These would be the "seat of the Government of the United States." The rest of the District would become the 51st state. Passage of this proposed legislation seemed unlikely at the end of the twentieth century. The district's status appeared likely to remain unchanged, with its residents subject to federal and D.C. taxes and federal laws, and with their having the right to vote for three electors for president and vice president.

The government of Washington in the late twentieth century, with an elected mayor and city council, operates under severe restrictions. It cannot, of course, tax the buildings of the federal government, which is the most valuable property in the District of Columbia. Nor can it tax the commuters who work in Washington but live in the Maryland or Virginia suburbs. Thus, the city government finds it difficult to raise revenue. Racial overtones are always present. Because the city government was scandal-ridden and short of funds throughout the 1990s, Congress took away some of Washington's limited power over its finances. In a related development, a proposed amendment to the Constitution to give the District of Columbia the right to elect voting representatives to Congress was not ratified.

ratify to formally approve a document, thereby making it legal

The Necessary and Proper Clause
Mark A. Graber

vest to grant with particular authority, property, and rights

ARTICLE I, SECTION 8, CLAUSE 18, OF THE CONSTITUTION STATES

*[The Congress shall have the Power] To make all Laws which shall be necessary and proper for carrying into execution the foregoing Powers, and all other Powers **vested** by this Constitution in the Government of the United States, or in any Department or Officer thereof.*

This last provision of Clause 18 in Article I, Section 8, authorizes Congress to pass laws needed in order to exercise its constitutional powers. It may seem to repeat other grants of power to Congress in the Constitution. Presumably, the seventh paragraph of Article I, Section 8, which gives Congress the power "to establish post offices and post roads," also gives it the power to pass laws establishing post offices and post roads. The same could be said for every other legislative power. Many Framers agreed that the necessary and proper clause was unnecessary. They claimed that the powers of Congress would be the same if the provision were not in the Constitution. The Anti-Federalists, who opposed ratifying the Constitution, often condemned that provision, which they thought would give absolute power to the national government. Similar debates over the constitutional meaning of the necessary and proper clause played a major role in American politics until after the Civil War.

Anti-Federalist member of the group opposing the adoption of the U.S. Constitution; favored states' rights and argued successfully for the Bill of Rights

Powers Granted to the National Government

Article I, Section 8, lists the powers granted to the national government. The first paragraph of that section gives Congress the "power to lay and collect taxes, duties, imposts and excises, to pay the debts and provide for the common defense and general welfare of the United States." Other clauses give Congress the power "to borrow money," "to regulate commerce with foreign nations," "to declare war," and "to establish uniform rules of naturalization." These powers were listed at length, because the Framers believed that the national government could exercise only those

duty a tax on goods brought into the country

impost an imposed charge; a tax or duty

excise a tax that a government puts on the manufacture, sale, or use of a domestic product

naturalization becoming a citizen

95

The 1787 historic pewter dollar–obverse (top) shows a sundial, the word "fugio," and the motto "Mind Your Business." The reverse (bottom) features thirteen interconnected rings, which, together with the "We Are One" lettering express national unity.

powers that were explicitly enumerated, or spelled out, in the Constitution. Supporters of the Constitution held that Congress had no power to punish people for practicing their religion or criticizing the government, because no constitutional provision authorized Congress to regulate religion or speech. In their view, the states retained the sole right to exercise any power that the Constitution did not specifically give to the national government.

The Constitution could not list every law the federal government could pass. Article I states that Congress has certain powers, but then allows Congress to decide how they should be exercised. For example, the power to "coin money" gives Congress the authority to determine whether quarters will be made of silver or copper, and to arrange to buy those metals. For this reason a law authorizing the president to buy silver for silver dollars is constitutional, even though the Constitution does not explicitly state that Congress has the power to purchase metal for coining money. The necessary and proper clause simply makes clear that the national government has the constitutional power to pass laws not mentioned in the Constitution whenever those laws help the government carry out powers that are mentioned in that document.

Americans continue to debate what policies are "necessary and proper" for carrying out governmental powers. Interpreted very loosely, almost any policy can be described as a necessary means of executing a legitimate government policy. Perhaps Congress could require that all teenagers follow a tough, daily three-hour exercise program on the grounds that this would help improve workers' productivity in the future, reduce health costs, and strengthen the national defense. Could Congress ban all criticism of government if such action would help the United States when it was fighting a "war"?

Yet if interpreted very narrowly, hardly any government policy can be described as necessary. Thus, while the Coast Guard provides many important services for Americans, is it absolutely necessary for the achievement of any national goal that Congress authorize the Coast Guard to exist? May the Congress empower the federal government to build federal prisons, or should persons who break federal laws be sent to existing state prisons?

Federalists Versus Anti-Federalists

Questions about the precise meaning of the necessary and proper clause are hard to answer, because the Framers did not give much thought to the meaning of this phrase. The delegates to the Constitutional Convention in 1787 seemed to regard "necessary and proper" as a rhetorical flourish and not worth debating. However, during the struggle over ratifying the Constitution, the meaning of the clause became a heated issue.

The Anti-Federalists, who opposed ratification, insisted that the necessary and proper clause was dangerous, because it would allow the national government to assume broad powers that were not specifically stated in the Constitution. The Anti-Federalists claimed that the clause could allow Congress to abolish people's liberties and even do away with

Federalist advocating a strong central government of separate states and the adoption of the U.S. Constitution

the states. The Federalists, who favored ratification, tried to calm concern about the clause by saying that it was not needed and merely gave Congress the power to pass laws that would carry out federal powers.

The Federalists won the debate over ratification, but only by agreeing that the Anti-Federalists had an important point. To ensure that Congress would not violate fundamental rights or interfere with state governments, the first Congress proposed the Bill of Rights. These first ten amendments of the Constitution were ratified in 1791. They make clear that the federal government must protect certain fundamental freedoms. The national government cannot limit free speech, conduct unreasonable searches, or violate other liberties, even when doing so might aid national defense or promote interstate commerce. The Tenth Amendment guarantees that state governments are to continue making important policies. That amendment declares, "The powers not delegated to the United States by the Constitution, nor prohibited by it to the states, are reserved to the states respectively, or to the people."

The Debate Over the Clause Continues

The ratification of the Bill of Rights did not end the debate over the meaning of "necessary and proper." When members of the second Congress proposed legislation to have the national government establish a national bank, President George Washington asked members of his cabinet whether that law was constitutional. Secretary of the Treasury Alexander Hamilton told President Washington that the act was constitutional, because a national bank would help the government regulate the

The Bank of the United States, chartered on February 25, 1791, under plans by Alexander Hamilton, was located in Philadelphia.

97

veto refuse to sign a bill into law

In *McCullough* v. *Maryland* in 1819, Chief Justice John Marshall wrote for a unanimous Court that Congress had the authority to charter a national bank. He adopted the view that Alexander Hamilton had advocated in the 1790s, that Congress had the power to adopt any measure related to the subjects that the Constitution mentions. In this way, Congress may exercise many powers not granted to it in so many words. "Let the end be legitimate," Chief Justice Marshall wrote, "let it be within the scope of the Constitution, and all means which are appropriate, which are plainly adapted to that end, which are not prohibited, but consist with the letter and spirit of the Constitution, are constitutional." As a result, the powers of Congress change with changing times.

see also

INTRODUCTION—Constitutional Concepts; ARTICLE I—Postal Power

★ **Congressional Investigations**
James Hamilton

vest to grant with particular authority, property, and rights

economy, pay its debts, and move money in times of war. Secretary of State Thomas Jefferson disagreed. He told the president that the necessary and proper clause did not permit the federal government to establish such a bank, because the government could still exercise all its powers even if no national bank existed. President Washington decided to accept Hamilton's advice and establish the bank. Then, twenty-five years later, in its very important decision in *McCulloch* v. *Maryland* (1819), the Supreme Court ruled that Washington was right—that the necessary and proper clause did give Congress the power to establish a national bank.

Still, the controversy over the clause continued. In 1833, President Andrew Jackson **vetoed** a bill to renew the charter of the national bank, because he did not believe the bank was necessary to any national power. Moreover, in the thirty years before the Civil War, many presidents vetoed bills providing for such things as federal roads and canals, improved navigation of rivers, hospitals for the mentally ill, financing education, and giving public land free to settlers. Those presidents vetoed such laws because they thought they were not necessary to carry out any power the government was constitutionally allowed to exercise.

At the close of the twentieth century, most people tended to agree with the view of the necessary and proper clause held by President Washington and Alexander Hamilton. Many politicians and legal scholars have thought that the national government should be allowed to pass any law that helps it exercise its powers as long as that law does not violate individual freedoms. However, many politically active citizens and elected officials have said that the federal government passes too many laws and that the states should do some of the things Congress does. Whether this critical view of the national government will result in an understanding of the necessary and proper clause more like Jefferson's is for future generations to determine.

ARTICLE I, SECTION 8, CLAUSE 18, OF THE CONSTITUTION STATES

[The Congress shall have the Power] To make all Laws which shall be necessary and proper for carrying into Execution the foregoing Powers, and all other Powers **vested** *by this Constitution in the Government of the United States, or any Department or Officer thereof.*

Nothing in the above provision gives Congress the power to conduct legislative investigations. Yet the Supreme Court has ruled that this power is part of the lawmaking powers the Constitution grants to Congress. Chief Justice Earl Warren noted, in *Watkins* v. *United States* (1957), "[The investigative] power is broad. It encompasses inquiries concerning the administration of existing laws as well as proposed or possibly needed statutes. It includes surveys of defects in our social, economic or political system for the purpose of enabling the Congress to remedy them. It comprehends probes into departments of the Federal Government to expose corruption, inefficiency or waste."

The Court's conclusion was not surprising because the authority of lawmaking bodies to conduct inquiries was well established when the Constitution was adopted. As William Pitt the Elder described the powers of Parliament in 1742, "We are called the Grand Inquest of the Nation, and it is our duty to inquire into every step of public management, either abroad or at home, in order to see that nothing has been done amiss."

Tools of Investigation

To investigate, Congress needs the power to compel testimony and the production of relevant documents. Congress issues subpoenas to accomplish this. Nothing in the Constitution gives Congress the right to issue subpoenas. But the Supreme Court has ruled that this authority is part of the legislative powers granted to Congress.

In 1927, in *McGrain* v. *Daugherty*, the Supreme Court ruled that "the power of inquiry—with process [that is, the subpoena power] to enforce it—is an essential and appropriate auxiliary to the legislative function." Again, in *Eastland* v. *United States Servicemen's Fund* (1975), the Court declared that "[t]he issuance of a subpoena pursuant to an authorized investigation is . . . an indispensable ingredient of lawmaking."

The reasons supporting an implied subpoena power are easy to understand. As the Court explained in the *McGrain* case, "A legislative body cannot legislate wisely or effectively in the absence of information respecting the condition which the legislation is intended to affect or change; and where the legislative body does not itself possess the requisite information—which not infrequently is true—recourse must be had to others who do possess it. Experience has taught that mere requests for such information often are unavailing, and also that information which is volunteered is not always accurate or complete; so some means of compulsion are essential to obtain what is needed."

The Court added that when the Constitution was adopted, the subpoena power was regarded as a necessary, appropriate, and inherent part of the power to legislate. This fact strengthened the Court's conclusion that the constitutional provisions placing the lawmaking function in the House and Senate were meant to give those bodies subpoena power.

Congress has passed laws to help carry out its constitutional powers to investigate. It has given itself the authority to place witnesses under oath who may be subject to prosecution for perjury if they lie. Congress also has passed a law allowing it to prosecute for contempt of Congress any person who defies a subpoena to testify or produce documents. Furthermore, both the House and Senate have the power to send their sergeant-at-arms to arrest and imprison any person who fails to comply with a subpoena, although Congress has not used this power since 1945. The Ethics in Government Act of 1978 gave the Senate, though not the House, the authority to bring a civil action against a person to force them to comply with a subpoena. But this act does not apply to federal employees who withhold evidence from Congress.

subpoena a court order requiring a person to appear to present testimony or documents

prosecution being charged with a crime and put on trial

perjury the willful breaking of an oath either by telling a lie or omitting to do what has been promised under the oath

contempt of Congress an action in direct violation of an order by Congress for which a person may be prosecuted

sergeant-at-arms an officer of Congress who preserves order and executes commands

civil action a lawsuit brought to protect a private or noncriminal right

Restrictions on Congress's Power

doctrine of legislative purpose a principle that Congress can investigate only matters that have a legitimate federal interest about which Congress has the power to legislate

Although Congress's powers to investigate are broad, they have certain limits, some of them imposed by the Constitution itself. The **doctrine of legislative purpose** gives some measure of protection to witnesses. Congress cannot investigate purely private matters just for the sake of exposing them. Nor can Congress hold legislative trials to convict and punish anyone by public rebuke or scorn. In the *Watkins* decision, the Court said that Congress is not a law enforcement agency or a trial court. The justices warned Congress against investigations undertaken just to gain publicity for its members or to punish individuals.

Yet the scope of the doctrine of legislative purpose is extremely broad. Congress legislates on a great variety of subjects, and the courts have recognized that the legislators act on the basis that they have a valid legislative purpose. The legitimacy of an investigation is not determined by its results. The very nature of an investigation means that it sometimes may lead lawmakers up some dead-end streets, as the Supreme Court declared in its 1975 *Eastland* decision. To be valid, a legislative inquiry does not need to end in a predicted result.

Congress's role in informing itself and the public about shortcomings and wrongdoings in government and other areas of federal interest is as important or perhaps even more important than its lawmaking role, President Woodrow Wilson once wrote. The Supreme Court also has recognized the importance of Congress's investigative role. Thus, the doctrine of legislative purpose may offer little real protection to persons under investigation by Congress when their mistakes or misdeeds are publicly revealed.

Witnesses' Rights

self-incrimination giving of testimony that will likely make a witness prosecutable

The Fifth Amendment protects witnesses against **self-incrimination**. That amendment, despite its wording, applies to Congress. It says that a person cannot be forced to give self-incriminating evidence in a criminal case. Even though a legislative investigation is not a criminal case, federal courts have ruled that this protection applies to congressional investigations.

immunity protection from legal action

Congress can get around the Fifth Amendment privilege and force witnesses to testify, even if this testimony is incriminating. Congress does this by invoking a federal law and obtaining a court order granting witnesses **immunity** from any prosecution using their testimony. But Congress usually does not rush to obtain immunity orders, because forcing a witness to testify may mean that the witness cannot be prosecuted later. In the 1987 Iran-Contra investigation by Congress, former White House staff members, Lieutenant Colonel Oliver North and John Poindexter, were required to testify under a grant of immunity. But their later convictions were overturned because the government could not show that the testimony they had given when granted immunity was not somehow used against them.

The Fourth Amendment protects witnesses against unreasonable searches, and thus against unreasonable subpoenas by Congress. But the Supreme Court ruled, in *United States* v. *McPhaul* (1960), that Congress has a broad leeway to investigate. So a congressional subpoena would have to be unreasonable to the point of being outrageous before the Court would rule it invalid.

Rules of Procedures

A congressional committee is allowed to seek only testimony and records that are related to its investigation. If a committee does otherwise, a witness cannot be convicted for contempt of Congress, even if that witness refuses to provide information. Furthermore, a person under investigation has a right to know why a question is being asked or why a requested document is relevant. The committee is obligated to explain its reasons.

In an investigation, a committee of Congress must follow its own rules and the rules of either the House or Senate that significantly affect a witness. If the rules are not followed, the witness may defy the committee without being in contempt. Again, this protection is not absolute. Even if a congressional committee fails to follow its rules, a witness's right to prevent such conduct by court action is limited. Why? The speech and debate clause of the Constitution in Article I, Section 6, is intended to guarantee lawmakers full freedom to enact legislation without being sued or harassed. This clause blocks a witness from suing a committee to stop a legislative investigation or to have it declared illegal.

The Importance of Investigations

There is no doubt that congressional investigations have had great importance over the years. Their impact sometimes has benefited the nation. Several such investigations exposed misdeeds and corruption at the highest levels of government. Among these were investigations into the

see also

ARTICLE I—The Impeachment Power;
Speech and Debate Clause;
FOURTH AMENDMENT—Unreasonable
Searches and Seizures;
FIFTH AMENDMENT—Right Against
Self-Incrimination

▶ The Senate committee organized to investigate the Watergate break-in holds a hearing in the Senate chambers, sometime during 1972–1974.

Congressional investigations sometimes provide high drama in American political life. One of those dramatic moments came in 1954, during hearings conducted by Senator Joseph McCarthy into charges that a Communist spy ring was operating at the United States Signal Corps installation at Fort Monmouth, New Jersey. These hearings were televised nationwide for over a month. Boston lawyer Joseph Welch represented the army. When Senator McCarthy made a vicious charge against one of Welch's assistants, Welch replied: "Until this moment, Senator, I think I never really gauged your cruelty or recklessness. . . . Have you no sense of decency, sir, at long last? Have you no sense of decency left?" McCarthy lost his power and influence not long after this incident.

Teapot Dome scandal in President Harding's cabinet in the 1920s and the Iran-Contra affair in the 1980s. In the 1970s, the Watergate investigation, headed by Senator Sam Ervin, led to the resignation of President Richard Nixon, criminal convictions of others, and an important overhaul of laws on campaign finances and ethics in government. During the Watergate investigation, the discovery of the White House tapes of President Nixon's conversations proved wrongdoing.

Other investigations have not been as worthwhile. In the 1940s and 1950s, congressional investigations into charges of Communist infiltration of government, universities, Hollywood film studios, and other institutions were often conducted in a glare of publicity. Committees abused witnesses, investigated charges unsupported by evidence, and conducted unlawful legislative trials. This period is often called the McCarthy era, because Senator Joseph McCarthy of Wisconsin headed a committee that came to symbolize this misuse of congressional power. Eventually, the Senate censured Senator McCarthy for his conduct. Even though in later decades witnesses were given more protections, the fairness of congressional hearings still very much depends on the character, judgment, and objectivity of the lawmakers conducting them.

★ Writ of Habeas Corpus
Barry Friedman

The privilege of the Writ of Habeas Corpus shall not be suspended unless when in Cases of Rebellion or Invasion the public Safety may require it.

The writ of habeas corpus is often called the "Great Writ" because of its important role in preserving individual liberty against government restraint. Article I, Section 9, Clause 2, of the Constitution provides that "The privilege of the writ of habeas corpus shall not be suspended unless when in cases of rebellion or invasion the public safety may require it." Despite this explicit provision in the Constitution, most habeas corpus cases in the nation's history have developed as part of statutory law rather than constitutional law.

statutory law law passed by legislators

Origins of the Great Writ

The writ of habeas corpus had its origins in Great Britain. The term *habeas corpus* in Latin means "to produce the body." This writ was a command by a court that the respondent, or the person to whom the lawsuit was directed (often a jailer), produce the person being held, so that a court could determine whether the person's detention was lawful. The writ of habeas corpus was designed from the beginning to protect people who had been deprived of their liberty. In its early years, the writ was used to keep royal officials and agents of the Crown from arresting people and imprisoning them without a trial.

"No doctrine involving more pernicious consequences was ever invented by the wit of man than that any [constitutional] provisions can be suspended during any of the great exigencies of government."

—Roger Brooke Taney (1777–1864), Chief Justice, U.S. Supreme Court

▶ Executive order 9066 and Public Law 503 (1942) made it possible for the government to evacuate from their homes, and relocate, persons of Japanese ancestry, thereby depriving them of their civil rights.

The meaning of the clause. Although the exact meaning of the habeas corpus clause in the Constitution is not entirely clear, the Framers agreed about its wording and importance. Their only disagreement seems to have been about how to make it more secure. Fortunately, there have been few cases in which to test this. Rarely has habeas corpus been suspended in American history, and usually it was in times of war.

Whose power? The most interesting constitutional question is whether the power to suspend the writ belongs solely to Congress, or if the president, too, has this power. Despite President Abraham Lincoln's decision to suspend the writ during the Civil War, the weight of history and authority suggests that the power is Congress's alone.

Uses of Habeas Corpus

In modern times, the writ of habeas corpus has mainly been used as a means of ensuring that criminal trials are free from constitutional error. In other words, courts use the writ to make certain that when the court finds a defendant guilty and sentences that person to prison or to death, it does so in a lawful fashion. Congress itself made this purpose clear when it passed a law in 1867 giving the federal courts the power to review the convictions of state prisoners to make sure they are lawful.

In habeas corpus cases, courts review many aspects of a criminal trial. They may hear prisoners' complaints that in getting their confessions, police officers violated their Fifth Amendment right not to be compelled to incriminate themselves. Likewise, a prisoner might come to a court seeking a writ of habeas corpus on the grounds that in his original trial police officers hid information important to the defense. Such violations do not, hopefully, happen very often, but when they do, the consequences are quite serious. Stated very simply, habeas corpus is a way of making sure that a criminal trial has been fair.

A Controversial Provision

Habeas corpus has become a controversial issue. One reason is that it is a sensitive matter whenever a federal judge reviews the work of a state judge, particularly if the federal judge releases a prisoner being held in a state prison. This is often considered to be a problem of federalism.

Another reason is that habeas corpus causes criminal proceedings to take longer. A defendant in a criminal case receives a trial, and then may appeal to a higher court (and even to the Supreme Court). Yet after all that, he or she may again come back to court, seeking a writ of habeas corpus. This situation is called the problem of finality. Some legal scholars argue that if criminal law is to be effective, challenges to convictions must come to a quick end. But despite the problems of federalism and finality, supporters of habeas corpus insist that the writ is essential to protect people from being unlawfully deprived of their liberty.

Perhaps the most significant reason the writ of habeas corpus has become controversial is its relationship to death penalty cases. When a criminal defendant has been sentenced to prison for many years, habeas corpus may drag out the legal proceedings for a long time, but the defendant remains in prison during the whole process. The defendant's punishment is not delayed. But if the prisoner has been sentenced to death, habeas corpus proceedings may delay an execution. For this reason, many people have argued that the right to habeas corpus should be limited.

Expanding Habeas Corpus

From about 1950 until the mid-1970s, the Supreme Court's rulings expanded the use of habeas corpus. Why this happened is not clear, but it occurred at the same time that many other rights of persons suspected of committing crimes also were expanded and strengthened. One of the Court's notable decisions in this period was *Mapp* v. *Ohio* (1961), which extended the Fourth Amendment's exclusionary rule against unlawful police searches and seizures. Another key ruling by the Court was *Miranda* v. *Arizona* (1966), which required police holding persons suspected of a crime to read them their rights before questioning them.

Narrowing Habeas Corpus

During the 1970s, the Supreme Court began to narrow the use of habeas corpus. Again, it is difficult to know precisely why, but at this time, many

federalism a system of political organization; a union is formed of separate states or groups that are ruled by a central authority on some matters but are otherwise permitted to govern themselves independently

see also

ARTICLE IV—States' Rights and
Federalism;
FOURTH AMENDMENT—Exclusionary Rule;
FIFTH AMENDMENT—*Miranda* v. *Arizona*;
Right Against Self-Incrimination;
EIGHTH AMENDMENT—Cruel and Unusual
Punishment

Americans were complaining that criminal suspects had too many rights, and that criminal proceedings dragged on far too long. The Supreme Court began to impose many limits on the use of habeas corpus. For example, it ruled that the writ of habeas corpus may not be used to complain that police violated the search and seizure protections of the Fourth Amendment.

The Court also ruled that prisoners may file only one habeas corpus petition unless they are able to prove that they are probably innocent of the crimes of which they were convicted.

Increased crime in the 1980s and early 1990s led Congress to become involved in the habeas corpus controversy. In 1996, it passed the Antiterrorism and Effective Death Penalty Act. Despite its name, much of this law was directed at limiting the ability of prisoners to obtain habeas corpus. The limitations under this law are complicated, although their restrictions are similar to those in rulings made by the Supreme Court in the 1980s and 1990s. Significantly, even though many people wanted it to do so, Congress refused to limit habeas corpus even more, remembering the important role of the Great Writ in protecting liberty.

Bills of Attainder
D. Grier Stephenson, Jr.

ex post facto law a law that punishes a person for an act which was not a crime at the time it was done

England had often resorted to bills of attainder for dealing with persons who had attempted, or threatened to attempt, to overthrow the government. In addition to the death sentence, attainder generally carried with it a "corruption of blood." This meant that the heirs of the person found guilty could not inherit his property. During the American Revolution, the legislatures of all the colonies passed laws directed against the **Tories**, including bills of attainder. The Framers of the Constitution adopted the provision outlawing them unanimously and without debate.

Tory any American who supported the efforts of the British crown against colonial independence during the American Revolution

ARTICLE I, SECTION 9, CLAUSE 3, OF THE CONSTITUTION STATES

*No Bill of Attainder or **ex post facto Law** shall be passed.*

A bill of attainder is a law that finds a person or persons guilty of a crime and sets their punishment without the safeguards of a trial by a court. The Framers forbade bills of attainder because they considered them to be the most serious threat to personal liberty. The ban on this practice is one of just a handful of limitations on power that the Constitution placed on the national government as well as the state governments.

The Supreme Court and Bills of Attainder

In English law, a bill of attainder originally referred to a legislative action ordering that persons named in the statute be put to death and forbidding their heirs from inheriting their property. A similar law, but one ordering less-severe punishments, was called a bill of pains and penalties.

From the nation's earliest history, American judges regarded attainder as any kind of punishment without trial. In 1810, in the case of *Fletcher* v. *Peck*, Chief Justice John Marshall described a bill of attainder in the United States as one that "may affect the life of an individual, or may confiscate his property, or may do both." In 1867, in *Cummings* v. *Missouri*, Justice Stephen J. Field ruled that a bill of pains and penalties was also a bill of attainder. In 1946, in *United States* v. *Lovett*, Justice Hugo Black stated that the ban here included all "legislative acts, no matter what their form, that apply either to named individuals or to easily ascertainable members of a group in such a way as to inflict punishment on them without a judicial trial. . . ."

Confederacy the eleven Southern states that seceded from the United States of America in 1860–1861

Elbridge Gerry (1744–1814) proposed a prohibition against bills of attainder at the Constitutional Convention of 1787. The measure passed unanimously.

draft the act of selecting for compulsory military service

Laws Ruled Bills of Attainder

In four cases, the Supreme Court has ruled a law to be a bill of attainder. One case (*Cummings* v. *Missouri* [1867]) was a Missouri law requiring certain professionals (in this case, a priest) seeking to practice their occupations to take an oath that they had never supported the **Confederacy**. Another case (Ex parte *Garland* [1867]) was a similar federal law that was applied to former members of Congress who wanted to practice law in the federal courts. A third case (*United States* v. *Lovett* [1946]) was a federal law that held back the salaries of three government employees who had been investigated by the House Committee on Un-American Activities. The fourth case (*United States* v. *Brown* [1965]) was a federal law that made it a crime for a member of the Communist party to serve as a labor union officer or be employed by a union in other than an unskilled job.

These cases illustrate that to be considered a bill of attainder, a law must do more than merely put a person or a group of persons at a disadvantage. The ban here is not a variation on the equal protection clause of the Fourteenth Amendment. Rather, three factors must be present if a law is, in fact, a bill of attainder: specification, or the naming of individuals or setting up a group of individuals from which there is no escape; punishment; and no trial by a court. These three factors also illustrate the discretion the Supreme Court has in deciding when a law crosses the line and becomes a bill of attainder.

Key Supreme Court Decisions

In *Hawker* v. *New York* (1898), the Supreme Court upheld a state law that barred persons convicted of a serious crime from practicing medicine. The justices ruled that the state's purpose here was not to punish but to prevent. In 1977, in *Nixon* v. *Administrator of General Services*, the Court rejected the former president's claim that the Presidential Recordings and Materials Preservation Act was a bill of attainder. The justices ruled that even though the law by name denied Nixon the right to keep his presidential papers even on a temporary basis, the burden, inconvenience, and disgrace that it imposed on him did not amount to a punishment.

A few years later, the Supreme Court considered another case claiming a law was a bill of attainder. In 1983, Congress passed a law that denied federal financial aid to any male student, age eighteen or older, who did not register for the **draft** with the Selective Service System. In *Selective Service System* v. *Minnesota Public Interest Research Group*, the Court ruled that withholding funds in such cases was not a bill of attainder. The draft law, the justices declared, did not specify the group of individuals whom it affected. Any student could remove himself from the group by obeying the law.

The ban against bills of attainder is consistent with the separation of powers doctrine of the Constitution. This ban says, in effect, that it is the job of the legislative branch, in response to public opinion, to make general rules that define what conduct is unlawful. At the same time, it is the job of the judicial branch, impartially and without regard to public opinion, to decide when someone has committed an illegal act. Thus, government may not punish someone until both Congress and a court have acted. The ban on bills of attainder also reflects the view, commonly held when the Constitution was written, that popular majorities represented by the legislature pose the greatest danger to the liberty of minorities.

Ex Post Facto Laws
Roger K. Newman

At the Constitutional Convention, two future Supreme Court justices, James Wilson and Oliver Ellsworth, argued that the prohibition of ex post facto laws was unnecessary. "There was no lawyer, no civilian who would not say that ex post facto laws were void of themselves," Ellsworth said. The clause was adopted by a divided vote on the argument that the colonies' unhappy experience with legislatures "overruled all calculations." This written prohibition was something "the judges can take hold of."

writ of habeas corpus (Latin, "produce the body") a court command to produce the person being held in order to determine whether the person's detention is lawful; a way of making sure that a criminal trial has been fair

ARTICLE I, SECTION 9, CLAUSE 3, OF THE CONSTITUTION STATES

No bill of Attainder or ex post facto Law shall be passed.

In Latin, the phrase *ex post facto* means "after the fact." The idea underlying a ban on ex post facto laws is that it is unfair to make illegal an activity that a person doing it did not know, and could not have known, was unlawful at the time it was done, for the simple reason that it was not illegal then. It is noteworthy that such laws were frequently found in ancient Greece and Rome and in early England.

Sir William Blackstone, the most important legal commentator of the eighteenth century, protested against ex post facto laws. Several state constitutions and declarations of rights prohibited passage of such laws, and other state constitutions also banned ex post facto laws, although they did not use this phrase to label them.

The Framers' View

The Framers of the Constitution considered this restriction on the legislature from passing ex facto laws so important that they imposed it on state governments in Article I, Section 10, Clause 2, as well as on the federal government in Article I, Section 9, Clause 3. Alexander Hamilton described the prohibition of ex post facto laws, along with the writ of habeas corpus and the ban against titles of nobility, as "perhaps greater securities to liberty and republicanism than any [the Constitution] contains." Ex post facto laws, he wrote in *The Federalist*, No. 84, "have been, in all ages, the favorite and most formidable instruments of tyranny." James Madison also discussed them in *The Federalist*, No. 44.

The Framers were divided, however, about whether the ban on ex post facto laws applied only to criminal laws and not civil laws. Several states during the period of the Confederation had passed paper money laws, which affected debts that were payable in gold and silver. Critics called them ex post facto laws. The Supreme Court considered the matter in 1798.

In that case, *Calder* v. *Bull*, Justice Samuel Chase wrote that there were four types of ex post facto laws. One type makes acts illegal that were not illegal when they took place. A second type makes the criminal act greater than it was when committed. Another type increases punishment for an illegal act after a person committed it. A fourth type changes the legal rules of evidence after the act took place to the disadvantage of the person charged.

Past Offenses and Future Privileges

Through the nineteenth century, the Supreme Court followed the definition of ex post facto laws in the *Calder* ruling as the sole definition. These principles were so widely accepted that in *Beazell* v. *Ohio* (1925), the Court summarized its definition of ex post facto in its ruling as "any **statute** which punishes an act previously committed, which was innocent when done; which makes more burdensome the punishment for a crime after its commission, or which deprives one charged with crime of any defense available according to law at the time when the act was committed is prohibited as ex post facto."

Under the ex post facto clause, a person who has committed certain past offenses can be denied certain privileges in the future. For example, a person may be denied the right to practice a profession. This can happen if the past offense itself, even though it took place before it was considered to be illegal, may be reasonably thought to continue to disqualify that person from the profession.

But the Supreme Court has held invalid a Missouri test oath that required persons holding public office, teachers, and preachers to swear that they had not sympathized with the South during the Civil War or aided its military forces. When a priest was **indicted** under this law, the Court heard the case. In its ruling in *Cummings* v. *Missouri* (1867), the justices declared the Missouri law unconstitutional, arguing that it did not relate to the priest's office or professional duties. The Court found that since it was not against Missouri law to sympathize with the South at the time of the Civil War, the state could not punish such conduct after the war by passing a law that applied to a period before the law was enacted.

Exceptions

The Supreme Court has consistently ruled that laws that change the punishment for an offense after it has been committed are ex post facto laws. An exception is sometimes made when the penalty is capital punishment, as the Court noted in *Dobbert* v. *Florida* (1977). Nor does a person on trial have a right to be tried using all legal procedures in effect when the crime he or she is charged with committing took place. But if a change in some trial procedures substantially changes the meaning of a crime, increases the possible punishment to the defendant, or denies the defendant a proper defense, the person being tried may use the ex post facto clause as a defense. These changes, however, cannot be used as a defense if the law has changed the legal procedures by which that person is being tried, as the Court ruled in *Collins* v. *Youngblood* (1990). Despite these exceptions, the ex post facto clause remains one of the pillars of constitutional government.

statute a law enacted by the legislative branch of government

indict to charge with a crime by a grand jury after it has examined the evidence and found that there is a valid case

▲ Justice Samuel Chase distinguished what has since become the accepted four kinds of ex post facto laws.

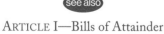

see also

ARTICLE I—Bills of Attainder

Contracts Clause
Stephen A. Siegel

treaty binding international agreement

letters of marque and reprisal documents issued by Congress (no longer used) that allowed private citizens to arm a ship and help American military forces; they helped by capturing enemy merchant ships and cargo, and by taking prisoners on land or at sea

contract a formal agreement, usually in writing, between two or more parties, that can be legally enforced

legislation the power and work of making laws

public contracts contracts to which a state is a party

Daniel Webster (1782–1852) served in Congress from both New Hampshire and Massachusetts, was a senator from Massachusetts, and twice was secretary of state. He gained much fame as one of the most eloquent advocates ever to appear before the Supreme Court, where he argued almost two hundred cases. Webster concluded his plea in the *Dartmouth College* case by stating, "It is, Sir, as I have said, a small college. And yet there are those who love it!" The philosopher Henry David Thoreau wrote, "God is only the president of the day, and Webster is his orator."

ARTICLE I, SECTION 10, CLAUSE 1, OF THE CONSTITUTION STATES

*No State shall enter into any **Treaty**, Alliance, or Confederation; grant **Letters of Marque and Reprisal**; coin Money; emit Bills of Credit; make anything but gold or silver Coin a Tender in Payment of Debts; pass any Bill of Attainder, ex post facto Law, or Laws impairing the Obligation of Contracts, or grant any Title of Nobility.*

The contracts clause in the Constitution provides that "No State shall . . . pass any Law Impairing the Obligation of Contracts." This provision prohibits the states from passing legislation that interferes with a **contract** existing when the law was passed. However, the contracts clause does not prohibit states from enacting legislation that changes contract law, effective in the future.

The Framers' intent. The Framers of the Constitution wrote the contracts clause to prevent states from passing debtor-relief laws. These laws allow persons owing money to postpone paying their debts, or to pay in installments, or to pay in kind rather than in cash. During the economic hard times following the American Revolution, the states passed numerous debtor-relief laws. Those laws were one of the chief grievances that spurred the Framers to replace the weak central government under the Confederation with a powerful national government. As James Madison wrote in *The Federalist*, No. 44, state interference with private contracts is "contrary to the first principles of the social compact, and to every principle of sound **legislation**."

The Court's interpretation. The significance of the contracts clause grew out of the early rulings of the Supreme Court under Chief Justice John Marshall that expanded its scope to include **public contracts**. In its decision in *Fletcher* v. *Peck* (1809), the Supreme Court relied on the contracts clause to overturn a law passed by Georgia's legislature that repealed grants of land the state had fraudulently been induced to make. The Court ruled that instead of enacting legislation, Georgia should have sued in court to cancel the land grants. The justices explained that in a judicial action, the rights of future buyers who purchased the land from the corrupt sellers would be protected.

The *Dartmouth College* Case

In the Supreme Court's 1819 decision in *Dartmouth College*, the justices once again expanded the contracts clause. In that landmark ruling, the Marshall Court ruled that corporate charters were within the scope of the contracts clause. This case began when one of the college's trustees appealed to the New Hampshire legislature to help him in a dispute with the other trustees. The legislature responded by passing a law increasing the size of the college's governing board and appointing enough new members to give the trustee a majority of votes on the board. Then members of the old board appealed to the federal courts, which voided the legislature's law. In its ruling, the Supreme Court declared that Dartmouth College's charter was a contract protected by the contracts clause, and thus prevented the state from controlling the college's affairs.

The *Dartmouth College* case had even greater importance when this ruling was applied to business corporations. Like Dartmouth College, business corporations originate in state-granted charters. In the early nineteenth century, business corporations were a new form of large-scale enterprise, and many soon became controversial because of their great power over competing businesses, their employees, and society in general.

In politics, Federalist and Whig leaders tended to favor protecting corporations' privileges. Republican and Democratic party leaders like Jefferson and Jackson tended to favor public regulation of corporations. When Chief Justice John Marshall, who was a Federalist, died in 1835, and Roger Taney, a Jacksonian, became Chief Justice, the Supreme Court suddenly reversed its view about the contracts clause's application to corporate charters.

The Taney Court's Decisions

In its decision in *Charles River Bridge* v. *Warren River Bridge* (1836), the Supreme Court said that even though corporate charters were within the scope of the contracts clause, they were to be interpreted strictly in favor of the public. No rights ever were to pass to corporations by implication. The Taney Court's view was quite different from the usual way contracts are interpreted. Contracts are interpreted even-handedly, without favoring either party involved, in an attempt to discover the parties' fair understanding of the agreement. This "strict constructionist" rule was the first of several rulings by the Taney Court that narrowed the contracts clause's protection of corporations.

Federalist advocating a strong central government of separate states and the adoption of the U.S. Constitution

Whig member of an American political party formed about 1834; associated chiefly with manufacturing, commercial, and financial interests

▼ In *Charles River Bridge* v. *Warren River Bridge* (1836), the Taney Court ruled that corporate charters were to be understood in favor of the public interest.

As the Taney Supreme Court cut back on the contracts clause's protection of corporations, it expanded the clause's restrictions on debtor-relief laws. In 1819, the Marshall Supreme Court had ruled that although the contracts clause prevented states from altering contract rights, the clause did not bar laws changing the judicial remedies by which contracts are enforced. Because contract rights depend on the remedies by which they are enforced, the " right-remedy" distinction clearly was a **loophole** in the clause's protection of contracts. While the Marshall Court recognized the potential danger of the "right-remedy" distinction, it never resolved it. However, the Taney Court closed this loophole. In the *Bronson* v. *Kinzie* (1842) decision, the justices ruled that the contracts clause forbade all retroactive changes in contract remedies that posed a burden on existing contract rights.

The different approach to corporation charters and debtor-relief laws by the Taney Court reflected the views of Jacksonian Democrats about private property and corporate wealth. Jackson and his party respected private property, but at the same time they feared the wealth produced by large-scale corporate businesses created by special state privilege.

loophole a means of evading or escaping an obligation or enforcement of a law or contract

Later Developments

After these rulings by the Marshall and Taney Courts, the contracts clause became the most litigated provision of the Constitution. That is, it was the provision most often challenged in state and federal courts. This clause also became the most frequent ground for overturning state laws. Above all, it became the Constitution's major protection for private property. By the early twentieth century, however, the contracts clause's importance declined as the Supreme Court turned to the doctrine of substantive due process to protect economic liberties.

Moreover, during the Great Depression, in *Home Building and Loan Association* v. *Blaisdell* (1934), the Supreme Court upheld state debtor-relief laws that the contracts clause originally had been written to prohibit. In its *Blaisdell* decision, the justices declared that the clause did not forbid reasonable changes in contract rights reached previously. This ruling came three years before the Supreme Court's retreat from protecting economic liberties under the substantive due process doctrine.

Since 1934, the Supreme Court has interpreted the contracts clause to prohibit only "unreasonable" interferences with contract terms. In keeping with modern constitutional law's declining protection for economic liberties, the Supreme Court has indicated that laws impairing contract rights are void only if they lack a rational, or reasonable, basis. The clause offers added protection only in cases in which states pass laws altering their own contracts. By the end of the twentieth century, the contracts clause no longer was a focus of constitutional debate or litigation.

ARTICLE I—Ex Post Facto Laws;
ARTICLE III—Judicial Review in the Nineteenth Century;
FIFTH AMENDMENT—Substantive Due Process

Article II

★ The Executive Branch

David Gray Adler and Michael A. Genovese

vest to grant with particular authority, property, and rights

George Washington takes the oath of office of First President of the United States on April 30, 1789.

*The executive Power shall be **vested** in a President of the United States of America. He shall hold his Office during the Term of four Years, and, together with the Vice President, chosen for the same term, be elected as follows:*

Each State shall appoint, in such Manner as the Legislature thereof may direct, a Number of Electors, equal to the whole Number of Senators and Representatives to which the State may be entitled in Congress: but no Senator or Representative, or Person holding an Office of Trust or Profit under the United States, shall be appointed an Elector.

The Electors shall meet in their respective States, and vote by Ballot for two persons, on whom one at least shall not be an inhabitant of the same State with themselves. And they shall make a list of all persons voted for, and of the Number of Votes for each; which List they shall sign and certify, and transmit sealed to the Seat of Government of the United States, directed to the President of the Senate. The President of the Senate shall, in the Presence of the Senate and House of Representatives, open all Certificates, and the Votes shall then be counted. The Person having the greatest Number of Votes shall be the President, if such Number be a Majority of the whole Number of Electors appointed; and if there be more than one who have such Majority, and have an equal Number of Votes, then the House of Representatives shall immediately chuse by Ballot one of them for President; and if no Person have a Majority, then from the five highest on the List the said House shall in like Manner chuse the President. But in chusing the President, the Votes shall be taken by States, the Representation from each State having one Vote; a quorum for this Purpose shall consist of a Member or Members from two-thirds of the States, and a Majority of all the States shall be necessary to a Choice. In every Case, after the Choice of the President, the Person having the greatest Number of Votes of the Electors shall be the Vice President. But if there should remain two or more who have equal votes, the Senate shall chuse from them by Ballot the Vice President.

The Congress may determine the Time of chusing the Electors, and the Day on which they shall give their Votes; which Day shall be the same throughout the United States.

No Person except a natural-born Citizen, or a Citizen of the United States, at the time of the Adoption of this Constitution, shall be eligible to the Office of President; neither shall any Person be eligible to that Office who shall not have attained to the Age of thirty-five Years, and been fourteen Years a Resident within the United States.

In Case of the Removal of the President from Office, or of his Death, Resignation, or Inability to discharge the Powers and Duties of the said Office, the same shall devolve on the Vice President, and the Congress may by Law provide for the Case of Removal, Death, Resignation, or Inability, both of the President and Vice President, declaring what Officer shall then act as President, and such Officer shall act accordingly, until the Disability be removed, or a President shall be elected.

The President shall, at stated Times, receive for his Services a Compensation, which shall neither be increased nor diminished during the Period for which he shall have been elected, and he shall not receive within that Period any other Emolument from the United States, or any of them.

Before he enter on the execution of his Office, he shall take the following Oath or Affirmation:— "I do solemnly swear (or affirm) that I will faithfully execute the Office of President of the United States, and will to the best of my Ability, preserve, protect, and defend the Constitution of the United States.

The American presidency was invented by the Framers of the Constitution. In creating this office, the delegates to the Constitutional Convention of 1787 drew upon their keen sense of history, the ideas of political philosophers and thinkers, their own political experiences, as well as practical considerations. But they were working from a blank sheet of paper, since the institution they were creating bore no resemblance to any previous executive model or office.

George Washington before the Constitutional Convention at Philadelphia, 1787.

The Issues at Hand

The Framers wrestled with many difficult questions, which included the following: Should the presidency be filled by one person (a single presidency) or by several persons (a plural presidency)? How should the president be elected—by the people, by Congress, or by some other means? What is the appropriate term that the president should serve? Should the president be eligible for reelection? Or is one term enough? Could the president be removed from office? And if so, by what means? Who should succeed a president who leaves office or dies before his term has expired?

The delegates to the Constitutional Convention also grappled with enormously difficult issues concerning presidential power. What kind of relationship should the president have with Congress? Should the president have a role in the legislative process? What role should the president play in formulating and conducting foreign policy and in war-making decisions?

These and related questions had to be considered within the structure of government the Framers were committed to: a government based on the doctrine of separation of powers. Essentially, the Framers wanted to avoid a monarchy. Throughout the Convention's proceedings, the delegates were determined to create an executive office in keeping with constitutional values.

The Framers, after all, had just fought the Revolution to free Americans from King George III, and they did not want to create a monarchy on American soil. Yet they understood the practical realities of government. They realized the need for a strong, independent, and vigorous executive who would enforce the laws and policies of Congress, and who also could provide a check on the legislative branch. Their mixed feelings about executive power influenced the way the Framers shaped the presidency and its powers.

The Vesting Clause

The first sentence of Article II, Section 1, of the Constitution is known as the vesting clause because it provides that the "executive power shall be vested in a president of the United States of America." The meaning of this clause has long been debated. Is it a grant of broad and general executive powers? Or is it just an expression that summarizes the specific presidential powers described after it, such as the veto, appointment, and pardon power? Scholars who take the broad view of the vesting clause argue that placing the executive authority of the nation in the presidency includes a "**prerogative**" power that enables the president to act in the absence of law or even to violate it in order to meet an emergency. But scholars who interpret the vesting clause narrowly argue that it merely introduces the presidential powers that are listed and fairly implied. They believe that the wording of the clause shows the Framers' decision to create a single rather than plural presidency, and that the title reflects the nation's chief executive.

The Framers' intent. There is little evidence to support the broader interpretation of the vesting clause. Indeed, the Framers feared the idea of an unrestrained or uncontrolled executive, vested with vast discretionary powers. One of the Framers' chief reasons for creating the presidency was the great need for an executive to enforce the laws. The "take care" clause of Article II, Section 3, charges the president with the solemn duty to "take care to faithfully execute the laws of the land." The somewhat awkward emphasis on the word "faithfully" probably stems from the fact that the British monarch enjoyed the **discretionary authority** to refuse to execute the laws of Parliament. The Framers wanted to make it crystal clear that the president would not be allowed such authority.

The duty to faithfully carry out the laws is hard to reconcile with the prerogative power. But apart from the debate over the vesting clause, the Framers clearly intended to establish a single rather than a plural executive and to call the holder of that office "president" rather than such alternatives as "excellency" or "supreme executive."

A single presidency. The Framers' preference for a single presidency reflects their emphasis on unified decision-making, accountability, and effective enforcement of laws and policies enacted by Congress. They believed that these presidential duties might be undermined by an executive council composed of several people with different interests, values, and

prerogative having to do with a special right or privilege particular to an office

discretionary authority power that may or may not be used

agendas, who could get bogged down in lengthy, fractious (unruly) debates. Rather than meet the need for strong leadership and accountability for actions taken in the executive branch, an executive council might well defeat this purpose, because it would be difficult to know who was responsible for abuses of power or incompetent acts.

Electing a President

The Framers saw the length of the president's term, eligibility for reelection, and the selection process to be closely connected. So they had to deal with these issues not individually, but in a comprehensive way. But the Framers' solution caused controversies at the Constitutional Convention and in later years as well. Indeed, Article II of the Constitution has been amended four times—more than any other part of the Constitution.

comprehensive including everything

Election process. In their consideration of the various issues involving the election of the president, the Framers faced continual problems. The delegates rejected a proposal for the direct, popular election of the president because they feared an uninformed electorate, and they wanted voting to be based on informed choices.

electorate those who have the right to vote in an election

Some delegates favored congressional selection of the president. They believed that the trusted representatives of the people might have personal knowledge of the candidates or could easily learn about their character, records, and qualifications. Such knowledge became all the more important when the Constitution's sole requirements for the office became that the president must be at least thirty-five years old, a natural-born citizen, and a resident for at least fourteen years. But the proposal that Congress elect the president complicated the issue. If the president were eligible for reelection and would be elected by lawmakers in Congress, he might be tempted to offer them bribes to ensure his reelection.

▶ Nelson Rockefeller, vice president of the United States in the Ford administration, announces the results of the Electoral College's ballots in the 1976 election. Jimmy Carter was elected president and Walter Mondale vice president.

115

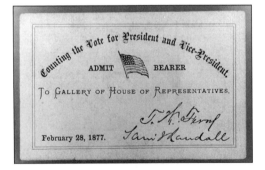

tenure length of time for holding a position or office

electoral college a body of people chosen by the voters in each state to elect the president and vice president of the United States

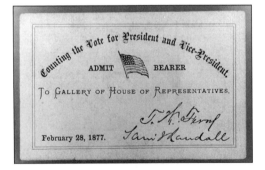

Admission ticket for entrance to the House chamber for the counting of the electoral vote in the contested election between Rutherford B. Hayes and Samuel J. Tilden. The joint session of Congress counted the votes on March 2, but tickets showing several dates had been printed in advance.

Reelection and duration of term. The issue of allowing a president to be reelected was itself complex, because it reflected different and conflicting values. The Framers favored the prospect of a president being reelected. They believed that it would provide motivation for good behavior and accountability (responsibility). It would also give the nation the benefit of presidential experience and expertise.

Yet, at the same time, the Framers recognized that longevity (a long duration) in office might lead to the abuse of power. So if the president were to be eligible for reelection, the term in office ought to be short. If the president were to serve only one term, then a longer tenure was preferable. In the end, the Framers' preference for an electoral college provided a workable solution to some of these problems.

The Electoral College

To capture the presidency, a candidate must win a majority of the electoral votes in the electoral college. Each state has a number of votes in the electoral college equal to its representation in Congress. The electoral college never meets. It serves only one function—to cast ballots in the election of the president (and vice president). When voters cast their ballots in a presidential race, they technically do not vote directly for a candidate but instead choose between slates of presidential electors. The slate of electors in each state is selected by the state political party and serves what is essentially an honorary role. The slate that wins the most votes throughout each state gets to cast all the electoral votes for the state. The electors on the winning slate travel to their state capital the first Monday after the second Wednesday in December and cast their ballots for their party's candidate. The ballots are sent from the state capitals to Washington, D.C., where the House and the Senate formally count them in early January, and the name of the next president is announced.

The role of Congress. If no presidential candidate wins a majority of the electoral votes, the election becomes the constitutional responsibility of the House of Representatives, which chooses the president from among the top three candidates. Each state delegation in the House has one vote. If no candidate wins a majority of the electoral votes in the election for vice president, the Senate chooses the vice president from one of the two top candidates. Each senator has one vote, and a majority vote is required to elect the vice president.

The Framers devised the electoral college in the hope that the best-qualified person would be elected president and the second-best-qualified candidate would become vice president. Confidence in the electors' judgment to choose wisely calmed the Framers' concerns about allowing a president to be reelected. And their concerns about the abuse of power if the presidential term was long were diminished by a term of four years—a tenure short enough to ensure presidential accountability.

The system's weakness. Despite the strengths of the electoral college system, it has some flaws and cracks that soon became clear. Perhaps the most fundamental problem was that the Framers did not foresee the rise

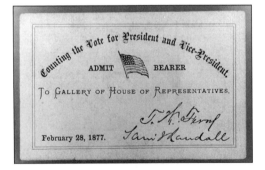

of political parties and could not know the impact party politics would have on the electoral college. In the election of 1800, Thomas Jefferson and Aaron Burr each received 73 votes in the electoral college. This tie vote threw the election into the House of Representatives, as the Constitution required. The House elected Jefferson president—but only after thirty-six ballots. The politics of mischief were clear, and many Americans feared similar abuses in the election of 1804. As a result, and despite the Framers' pride in their creation, the electoral college became the first governmental institution to be amended.

The Twelfth Amendment, ratified in 1804 before the election, provides for separate balloting for president and vice president by the electoral college. The Twenty-second Amendment, ratified in 1951, prohibits any person from being elected president more than two times. This amendment overturned the Framers' decision to permit a person to seek an unlimited number of terms in office.

Removal from Office

The delegates to the Constitutional Convention faced the issue of removing a president from office. A presidential abuse of power might require removal, and **impeachment** was the remedy. There was also the question of a president's disability. What if the president becomes ill and is no longer able to perform the duties of the office? The possible disability, death, or resignation of a president raised the question of succession.

The Constitution's wording left these matters in doubt. For example, "disability" was not defined, and there was no provision for determining how the powers of the office ought to be transferred to a successor. The Twenty-fifth Amendment, ratified in 1967, provided that when a president is removed from office, the vice president becomes president. It also established a process to deal with presidential disability.

Presidential Salary

As part of the doctrine of the separation of powers, the Framers sought to protect the president's independence against bribes or financial threats in much the same way that they had protected the judiciary. The Framers provided that the president's salary could neither be increased nor decreased during his term of office. They also prohibited the president from receiving compensation from any state.

The Vice President

Creating the office of vice president raised little controversy at the Constitutional Convention. The delegates were familiar with the practice under British rule, when the colonies had lieutenant governors with few powers other than to succeed the governor upon his death. The delegates also knew that, after independence, in several states different officials succeeded to the governorship in the event of death or resignation. But the delegates never referred to the position of lieutenant governor in

impeachment method by which the House of Representatives may charge the nation's highest-ranking officials, including the president, with wrongdoing; and following impeachment, if the officials are found guilty of the charges, the Senate then may try them and remove them from office

Throughout American history, vice presidents have served mainly as presidents of the Senate. Often dismissed as an unimportant office without significant duties, or as a stepping-stone to the presidency filled by a person waiting for the president to die, the vice presidency was often seen as a joke.

According to Lyndon Johnson, who served as President John Kennedy's vice president, the vice president "is like a raven, hovering around the head of the president, reminding him of his mortality." But the Twenty-fifth Amendment, by its two-term limit for any one president, has made it easier for a vice president to become a candidate for president. More important, starting with the administration of President Jimmy Carter in 1977, vice presidents have assumed greater policy-making responsibilities, especially in domestic affairs.

see also

ARTICLE II—Enforcing the Laws; Presidential Qualifications, Succession, Pay, and Oath; TWELFTH AMENDMENT; TWENTY-SECOND AMENDMENT; TWENTY-FIFTH AMENDMENT

▲ President Bill Clinton and Vice President Al Gore at the White House (1993).

Presidential Emergency Powers
Christopher H. Pyle

authority the power to grant legal allowance

debates, and thus it is difficult to know whether that office had much influence on the Framers' thinking. In fact, the proposal to establish the vice presidency was not made until very late in the Convention's proceedings. The creation of the office seems to have resulted from the difficult issues the Framers faced in the selection of the president. In a sense, the vice presidency was a kind of necessary institution.

Selection of the vice president. The Framers' decision to establish the electoral college raised other significant problems. The possibility existed that electors might vote for local candidates, which would deprive the country of a nationally selected president. The Framers solved this problem by allowing electors to cast two votes, but required that the electors cast one of the votes for someone who "shall not be an inhabitant of the same state with themselves." The delegates also provided that the runner-up in electoral votes would become vice president. This provision settled the problem of the role of the president of the Senate.

Presiding over the Senate. For various reasons, the Framers did not want a senator to be president of the Senate. They decided that the vice president was to preside over the Senate but to vote only when it was necessary to break ties. Finally, creating the vice presidency resolved the question about succession to the presidency.

The Constitution assumes that Congress will pass laws giving the president authority to act on behalf of the United States. The process was meant to be a slow, complicated one, so that members of Congress would think carefully about giving the president too much power.

The Constitution is less clear about the president's power during major emergencies, such as rebellions and foreign invasions, when there is no time for Congress to give the president special powers. The constitutions of some countries give their leaders authority to suspend the normal operation of the laws in order to deal with grave threats to the nation's domestic or national security. Many political leaders, including German dictator Adolf Hitler, have used such emergency powers to imprison their opponents and establish dictatorships.

The Framers of the Constitution understood how emergency powers could be abused. Britain's decision to place rebellious Boston under military rule in 1775 triggered the outbreak of the American Revolution. The Constitution does not empower the president to disregard ordinary laws, including those protecting individual freedoms, in order to deal with emergency threats to the nation's security from spies and saboteurs, or from those plotting rebellion.

Suspending Habeas Corpus

The Constitution does allow the federal government to take certain actions during emergencies. Article I, Section 9, Clause 2, allows it to

writ of habeas corpus (Latin, "produce the body") a court command to produce the person being held in order to determine whether the person's detention is lawful; a way of making sure that a criminal trial has been fair

"suspend the privilege of the **writ of habeas corpus**." Under this legal procedure, persons who are arrested can go to court and win release by showing that the government lacks legal authority to hold them. But the power to suspend that procedure can be used only "in cases of rebellion or invasion," and even then, only when "the public safety may require it." Moreover, the Constitution gives this dangerous power to Congress, not the president. Thus, if the president believes that the military should have the power to round up enemy sympathizers in time of war, he must first go to Congress and get permission to order this action.

President Lincoln's Actions

Despite the constitutional protection of habeas corpus, two presidents have imprisoned thousands of persons during wartime without trial. Early in the Civil War, President Abraham Lincoln ordered the detention of hundreds of suspected Southern sympathizers, including members of the Maryland legislature. Lincoln acted on his own authority, but later Congress passed a law allowing such arrests, and thousands more were imprisoned. His Secretary of State, William H. Seward, boasted that he could ring a little bell on his desk and order that any person in the United States be put in prison without a trial. Not until after the Civil War ended did the Supreme Court, in *Ex parte Milligan* (1866), overturn the government's excessive use of this power.

inherent power power belonging to the office (i.e., the presidency) but not spelled out in the Constitution

President Franklin D. Roosevelt's Actions

Following Japan's attack on Pearl Harbor, President Franklin D. Roosevelt ordered the roundup and detention of 110,000 persons living on the Pacific West Coast of the United States. Most of those detained were of Japanese ancestry, and the army feared that they might help the Japanese navy launch another sneak attack, this time on the mainland. In taking this step, President Roosevelt at first claimed an **inherent**, not an expressed, constitutional **power** to do so. Soon afterward, Congress authorized his action. The army claimed it had secret evidence that these imprisonments were necessary, when in truth it had none. Nor did the courts demand any such proof until the war was nearly over.

In early 1942, shortly after Congress declared war against Japan, President Franklin Roosevelt signed an executive order authorizing the removal of all persons of Japanese ancestry from most of the West Coast. Approximately 110,000 people, largely native-born American citizens, were ordered to sell every possession. They were rounded up and detained in remote areas in western states, living in tar-paper barracks heated with coal stoves. Military police armed with rifles guarded them. Even Roosevelt later called them "concentration camps." The Supreme Court upheld the evacuation in 1944 and most of the internees were released late that year. A congressional committee in 1983 reported that the internment was a "grave injustice" prompted by "racial prejudice, war hysteria, and failure of political leadership." In 1988 Congress passed a law giving $20,000 and an apology to each of the surviving internees.

In summary, even though the Constitution may forbid mass roundups in response to wartime fears, two presidents were able to carry out such actions. They were able to do so in large part because Congress and the public believed that the president needed nearly unlimited power to win a war that threatened the very survival of the nation.

President Truman's Failed Attempt

The case was different when President Harry S. Truman took similar action during the Korean War of the early 1950s. The nation's survival was not threatened, but when a labor dispute in steel mills threatened to halt production of military weapons, President Truman ordered troops to seize the mills. The owners went to court, and the Supreme Court ruled

 A Japanese family sits with their belongings as they wait for transport to an internment camp where they will be confined for the duration of World War II. San Francisco, 1942

in their favor, in *Youngstown Sheet & Tube Co.* v. *Sawyer* (1952). The Court ordered Truman to give back the mills because he had failed to obey a law telling how the president should deal with such strikes. Even so, if the law had not existed, or if the emergency had been more serious, most of the justices would have upheld the president's action. This suggests that the president's vague powers as chief executive and as commander in chief may, in fact, allow him to override citizens' constitutional rights in serious military emergencies.

The Reality of the Emergency Powers

If the threat to the nation seems great enough, neither Congress nor the courts are likely to block actions taken by a strong-willed president. In such an emergency, the president will do whatever seems required, politically or militarily, without worrying very much about the Constitution or the law. His lawyers will defend such actions by pointing to the vagueness of the executive powers granted in Article II as well as to any emergency laws Congress may have passed in earlier crises and forgotten to repeal. While these claims are being debated in Congress and the courts, the president's controversial action will continue, and then the president will ask Congress to authorize what he has already done.

What will be the outcome of the president's request in Congress? If its members oppose what the president has done, they may choose to do nothing and let him be sued in court, as they did in the case of the steel-mills seizure. If members try to overturn the president's actions, however, they will quickly discover that he has many supporters in Congress eager

repeal revoke or cancel

legislation the exercise of the power and function of making laws

veto refuse to sign a bill into law

national guard the organized militia in each state or territory; at the same time a reserve of the United States army or air force

appropriate set aside for or assign to a particular purpose or use

to delay **legislation**. If both houses of Congress pass a law limiting the president's authority, he can **veto** it. Rarely can Congress muster a two-thirds vote in both houses to override a presidential veto. Meanwhile, anyone who brings a court challenge of the president's use of emergency powers can expect government lawyers to use every possible means to prevent any judicial decision until the crisis is over. Judges may allow delays, fearing to undermine the government during a crisis or to have their orders defied.

Laws of Congress, not provisions in the Constitution, give presidents the power to use the military to deal with riots, strikes, and natural disasters. In such emergencies, the local police and the state **national guard** have the duty to act first. Only if they cannot handle the crisis may the president send in troops. Even then, presidents rarely do so until the governor of the state has requested federal troops, as was the case in the urban rioting of 1967 and 1968, or when those troops are needed to enforce a court order, as in the desegregation of Central High School in Little Rock, Arkansas in 1957.

Other Presidents and the Emergency Powers

Presidents often have acted alone during times of emergency. Thomas Jefferson once spent money not **appropriated** by Congress to buy gunpowder because he feared a British attack. However, he admitted he had acted without authority and promptly sought approval from Congress. Other presidents have been less candid, preferring to claim broad powers and daring Congress and the courts to disagree. Lincoln, for example, argued that the Constitution, as if magically, gives the president all the war powers he needs in times of emergency without the need for any additional authority or any appropriation of money from Congress. Even so, despite these claims, he did eventually seek authority from Congress for his actions. Lincoln also conceded that once the emergency of the Civil War was over, his dictatorial use of power would end.

Theodore Roosevelt was much bolder in claiming power. He insisted that the president always has the power to do whatever is needed for the good of the country unless it is expressly forbidden by the Constitution or laws. President Truman, too, acted in a similar manner. In 1950, he justified his decision to send troops to defend South Korea without Congress's authority, first by refusing to call this conflict a war, and then by suggesting that the United Nations (a body not even conceived of in the Constitution) had somehow given him authority for his action. However, once American troops were fighting in Korea, Congress found it impossible politically to oppose the president.

The Cold War and National Security

During the Cold War (1945–1989), some high officials declared that the United States faced a permanent national security threat. They believed that this gave the president nearly unlimited power to order secret military operations against Communist nations without Congress's knowledge or permission. Such actions were in violation of United States law as well as foreign and international law. Nevertheless, some of the secret operations grew into large-scale warfare. One became the Vietnam War, which involved over one half million soldiers.

As part of government planning to safeguard the nation's security during the Cold War, the executive branch in the 1950s secretly built emergency detention camps and secretly compiled a list of thousands of persons it suspected of disloyalty. Those persons were to be rounded up and held without trial in case of a conflict with the Soviet Union or China. During the early 1970s, President Richard M. Nixon claimed that he could secretly order the Federal Bureau of Investigation, the Central Intelligence Agency, and military intelligence to spy on and harass Americans who protested against the Vietnam War. Nixon declared such action was lawful because "when the president does it, that means it is not illegal." However, when Nixon's staff ordered the burglary of the offices of the Democratic National Committee at the Watergate office building, no such broad claims of emergency power could prevent his being forced from office.

In short, the president's authority to deal with emergencies, whether real or alleged, is based more on laws passed by Congress than on the vague language of Article II outlining presidential powers. In times of war, presidents have violated both the Constitution and the laws for months, even years, confident that neither Congress nor the courts were likely to interfere. The main limits on presidential power in emergencies, then, are more likely to be political than legal.

see also

ARTICLE I—Writ of Habeas Corpus;
ARTICLE II—National Security and the Presidency; Steel Seizure Case

★ Steel Seizure Case
Nancy Kassop

inherent power power belonging to the office (i.e., the presidency) but not spelled out in the Constitution

authority the power to grant legal allowance

injunction an order issued by a court

stay stop

veto refuse to sign a bill into law

The steel seizure case presented the Supreme Court with the issue of whether a president has inherent executive power to act in an emergency. President Harry S. Truman took over the nation's steel mills in April 1952 in order to head off a major strike, at a time where there was a continuing need for steel production to supply American military forces in Korea. In *Youngstown Sheet and Tube Co.* v. *Sawyer* (1952), the Court, in a 6-to-3 decision with five separate concurring opinions, rejected President Truman's sweeping claims of his power as president to take private property without authority from Congress. The Court rebuked the president for usurping legislative power and for acting against the expressed intent of Congress.

Seizing the Steel Mills

Upon the announcement in April 1952 that all work would immediately stop in the nation's steel plants, President Truman issued an executive order to Secretary of Commerce John Sawyer to seize the mills and operate them. Truman cited his power under the Constitution and laws as president and commander-in-chief as authority for his action. He reported the seizure to Congress twice, but Congress took no action.

injunction an order issued by a court

stay stop

veto refuse to sign a bill into law

The steel company's lawyer, John W. Davis, told the justices that Truman's action was not only a "usurpation" of power, not only a deed "without parallel in American history," but "a reassertion of the kingly **prerogative**, the struggle against which illumines all the pages of Anglo-Saxon history." At the end of his argument Davis looked up at the ceiling in the Supreme Court and in a low voice quoted Jefferson, "In questions of power let no more be said of confidence in man, but bind him down from mischief by the chains of the Constitution." President Harry Truman strongly disagreed. He felt that the case was his "Dred Scott decision," a "crazy decision that has tied up the country" and that "seriously hamstrung" the presidency.

prerogative having to do with a special right or privilege particular to an office

veto refuse to sign a bill into law

The steel companies sued the president in federal court, asking for **injunctions** to stop the seizure of the mills and for a ruling declaring the executive order unconstitutional. The lower court decision granted the companies' requests, but the Court of Appeals **stayed** the decision. Within three days, the Supreme Court agreed to hear the case, and handed down its decision only one month later.

At the heart of the case was the fact that the president could offer no law as authority for his action. Equally important, when Congress passed the Taft-Hartley Act in 1947, it had considered giving the president power to seize industries during emergencies, but had expressly decided not to do so. Also, President Truman could have used existing provisions in the Taft-Hartley Act that called for a sixty-day cooling-off period or two other acts of Congress that gave the president limited power to act in such emergencies.

Instead, he defended his actions in court by claiming that they were "implied from the aggregate of his powers under the Constitution." President Truman relied on three clauses in Article II: the executive power clause of Section 1, the commander-in-chief clause of Section 2, and the "take care" clause of Section 3.

The Supreme Court's Decision

Justice Hugo Black, in his opinion for the Court, strongly rejected each of the sources of authority the president claimed. He dismissed the use of the commander-in-chief clause by noting that the power to seize property in labor disputes was "a job for the Nation's lawmakers, not for its military authorities." He rejected the "take care" clause by declaring that the president's power under this clause "refutes the idea that he is to be a lawmaker." Finally, Truman's action could not be justified as an act of "executive power," since, in Black's words, "the Constitution is neither silent nor equivocal about who shall make laws which the President is to execute." He pointed out that Article I grants all legislative power to Congress, while the Constitution limits the president's functions to recommending and **vetoing** laws.

The dissenting opinion by Chief Justice Fred Vinson argued that the president's actions were temporary ones, taken during an emergency and intended to protect other laws of Congress. According to Vinson, the president was executing the laws, which presidents could do without a specific law passed by Congress saying so.

The Case's Legacy

The steel seizure case has left a mixed legacy. To be sure, it puts presidents on notice that their actions are not free from judicial review. It also makes it clear that there is a limit on how far presidents can act during emergencies without congressional authorization, and where Congress's expressed or implied intent is known. It is a less clear guide as to how the Court would view a similar use of presidential power during emergencies in which Congress's intent was not known or not expressed. Only two members of the Court, Justices Black and William O. Douglas appeared to reject any emergency power for the president. Four other justices in their concurring opinions recognized a one-sided presidential power when it did not conflict with Congress, and the three justices in dissent approved the president's actions. So the Court's decision in *Youngstown Sheet and Tube Co.* v. *Sawyer* in reality leaves presidents with more flexibility to act than the ruling on its face might suggest.

The immediate and very practical result was that the Court curbed President Truman's power to act in this particular emergency. Yet it also appeared to accept the existence of such a power if the emergency was grave enough and if Congress had not already acted. The most lasting lesson of the steel seizure case is found in the warning in Justice Robert H. Jackson's cautionary opinion: "We may say that power to legislate for emergencies belongs in the hands of Congress, but only Congress itself can prevent power from slipping through its fingers."

see also

ARTICLE II—National Security and the Presidency; Presidential Emergency Powers

National Security and the Presidency
Morton H. Halperin

If the nation's survival is at stake, do the Constitution's restrictions on the power of the president no longer apply? When crises occur, can presidents do whatever they believe is necessary to protect the nation's security? This is the central issue in the debate about the relationship between the presidency and national security.

The Framers of the Constitution recognized that sometimes the nation would need to act with "secrecy, vigor, and dispatch," that is, quickly and quietly, especially when dealing with threats from other nations. They decided, therefore, to make the presidency consist of a single person, believing that an individual could act more swiftly and decisively than a group in emergencies. At the same time, they feared placing all the executive power in one person, who could then abuse it. Therefore, they gave many national security functions to Congress. The Framers' decisions have been viewed in different ways ever since.

Arguments in Favor of Presidential Power

The president is both commander-in-chief of the armed forces and the spokesperson for the United States in foreign affairs. Americans tend to view the president's authority in these two roles in different ways. Some argue that the president has very broad powers and that these powers increase greatly during a time of emergency, such as an armed attack on the United States. They claim that the president does not need the consent or agreement of Congress to act when he or she believes the nation's security is threatened. Instead, the president can react alone to the crisis. For example, he might decide to order American troops into battle in order to defend the United States against an attack. Congress and the courts, under this view, have little power to limit the president's actions as commander-in-chief, and the courts must use their powers to direct others to obey presidential orders.

Arguments Against Presidential Power

Those who hold the contrary view argue that the president's powers do not increase when national security issues are involved. They believe that, in most cases, Congress must first pass laws that **authorize** an action before the president can execute it, and that even when the president is acting with Congress's approval, the chief executive must still respect the rights of individuals as spelled out in the Constitution and the Bill of Rights. The president alone cannot decide to send American forces into combat without congressional approval simply because he or she believes that the nation's security is threatened, these commentators claim. They also feel strongly that the courts have the power, as well as a duty, to enforce these limits on presidential actions.

authorize grant legal allowance to

The Supreme Court's View

Just as the Framers left this issue of presidential power unresolved, so has the Supreme Court. The Court considers four factors in deciding when a president's actions are justified during a national crisis: (1) whether the action falls clearly within the president's powers as defined by the Constitution; (2) whether there is a national emergency, and if so, what kind; (3) whether the action affects individual rights; and (4) whether Congress has indicated how it believes the crisis should be handled.

Constitutional Provisions

Surprisingly, the Constitution grants the president only a few powers relating to national security. It makes the president the commander-in-chief of the army and navy. It authorizes the president to make **treaties** with other countries, but requires that they be approved by a two-thirds majority of the Senate. The Constitution empowers the president to appoint high government officials, military officers, and ambassadors, but, again, only with the Senate's consent. Finally, it allows the president to receive ambassadors from other countries on his own.

treaty binding international agreement

In contrast, the Constitution gives extensive national security powers to Congress. Not only do treaties and presidential appointments require Senate approval, but the Constitution grants Congress the power to declare war, to raise and support armies, to appropriate funds for the armed forces, and to enact rules for military operations.

Nevertheless, despite the clear language of the Constitution, the courts and the American people have tended to view the president's powers as extremely broad when it comes to protecting the national security. They believe that the role of commander-in-chief authorizes the president to dispatch American troops abroad and even to send them into combat. They also think the president has the power to take strong actions at home as long as these are "necessary in the national interest." A concern for individual rights and the separation of powers between Congress and the president reasserts itself in calm times. In this way, the issue remains unresolved. Presidents and their supporters tend to stress

The president's chief foreign policy adviser, according to what presidents say and according to formal laws, is supposed to be the secretary of state. Since the 1960s, however, the president's national security adviser has rivaled the secretary in influence. This is partly due to nearness to the president—the national security adviser is just down the hall in the White House. Presidents grow to rely on these aides: They believe that the adviser owes his prime political loyalty to the president, and not to any department or program. Each president shapes the adviser's job to suit his own personal preferences. They see and talk with each other at least once daily. The adviser has a major role in both making and implementing foreign policy.

The most famous national security adviser was Henry Kissinger, who served Presidents Richard Nixon and Gerald Ford while also serving as secretary of state for part of the same time. A brilliant former Harvard professor, Kissinger functioned, especially under Ford, as sort of deputy president of foreign affairs. As one journalist wrote, Kissinger had "created a new power center not accountable to anyone but the president."

infringe exceed the limits of, or violate

the dangers in security situations because these justify more extensive presidential powers. People concerned with civil liberties and congressional power may question the security threat and stress the need to examine carefully claims that the nation's survival is at stake.

Protecting Individual Rights

Many presidential actions during times of crisis do not infringe on individual rights, but when they do, the courts carefully examine those actions to determine whether they are constitutional. One of the most serious conflicts between individual rights and presidential power in the name of national security occurred during World War II, when the United States was at war with Japan. President Franklin D. Roosevelt's advisers persuaded him that Americans of Japanese ancestry were a threat to the nation's security. As a result, the government removed Japanese Americans, both citizens and noncitizens, from their homes and forced them to relocate into internment camps. The Supreme Court upheld this action. Several decades later, in the 1980s, Congress apologized for this action on behalf of the United States and offered compensation to those who had been sent to these camps.

Another conflict between claims of protecting national security and individual rights came during the Nixon administration, in 1972. The administration asked the courts to prevent the publication of what became known as the Pentagon Papers, a secret history of the Vietnam War written in the Defense Department in the closing years of the preceding Johnson administration. The government claimed that publishing these documents, which it charged were "stolen," would harm the president's ability to fight the war effectively and to negotiate a settlement of the conflict. But two of the nation's leading newspapers, *The New York Times* and *The Washington Post,* refused the government's request to stop publication and to return the documents. The Supreme Court ruled against the government, declaring that the likely result of publishing the documents was not serious or immediate enough to justify ordering the papers to stop publication.

The Pentagon Papers decision was considered a great victory for the press and for those who believed that presidential power needed to be limited. In later rulings, the Court showed much more sympathy to government claims that national security was at stake. Ironically, since the end of the Cold War, the courts have given the president greater freedom to act in ways that adversely affect individual rights. This has been particularly true for certain groups of people, such as those seeking to enter the United States illegally.

President Truman's Seizure of the Steel Mills

Another famous face-off between the emergency powers of the president and the rights of citizens took place in 1952, during the Korean War. This was not a declared "war" but a United Nations police action in which the United States was heavily involved. When steelworkers threatened to strike, President Harry S. Truman ordered the government to gain possession of the steel mills and directed the workers to remain on the job on the grounds that a strike would threaten the production of weapons for American soldiers in Korea. The owners of the steel plants sued the government. The Supreme Court, in *Youngstown Sheet & Tube Company* v. *Sawyer* in 1952, ruled the government's action to be unconstitutional. This is its most important ruling in limiting the president's national security powers.

The Supreme Court's Ruling

Justice Robert Jackson wrote an important concurring opinion in which he described several possible national security situations and suggested that the president's powers vary in each of them.

The First Situation: When the president acts after a clear or suggested delegation of powers by Congress

In this situation, presidential authority is greatest, since the president is acting under the power to protect the nation's security that the Constitution grants separately to both the president and Congress. The Supreme Court will usually take a very expansive view of this issue and, at least in the area of national security, will rule that Congress can delegate any of its powers to the president. In fact, the Court has found that the only limitation on presidential authority in these circumstances is when the action violates individual rights in a way that is not permissible, even given the severity of the threat to national security.

Moreover, the Court has regarded some congressional actions as a clear delegation of authority to the president. During the Vietnam War, for example, the Court held that by appropriating money for the armed forces without limitations, Congress, in effect, had authorized the president to conduct military operations. The Court ruled in this way even though the Constitution grants the power to declare war to Congress, not to the president.

The Second Situation: When the president acts in a situation where Congress has taken no action at all

In this situation, the president's powers are less clear. However, Justice Jackson suggested that the president may have greater ability to act if Congress has failed to decide how the nation should respond to a given threat but has not delegated its powers to the president. The Court confirmed this view in later decisions.

The Third Situation: When Congress has acted and indicated what course should be followed in a particular emergency

In this situation, the president has limited power to take a different action from that which Congress has specified. This was the case when the government took over the steel mills during the Korean War. It probably also explains why the Court refused to uphold President Truman's actions.

A papier-mache figure of President Richard Nixon at a Pentagon Papers demonstration

President George Bush, General Colin Powell and top military advisers discuss Operation Desert Storm, a military strike that Congress had not authorized when the president sent troops to Kuwait.

A meeting of the National Security Council's Executive committee during the Cuban missile crisis (1962). The committee met in President Kennedy's cabinet room.

Before the steel mill takeover, Congress had passed the Taft-Hartley Law, which provided that in times of emergency, the president could end a strike by ordering a "cooling off" period. During this time, the president was supposed to try to mediate an end to the dispute. President Truman did not want to use this authority because organized labor did not like the law and considered it antiunion legislation. The Supreme Court took a different view, and ruled that in cases where Congress had laid out a way to act to approach a crisis, such as in the Taft-Hartley Law, the president must follow it unless the Constitution clearly authorizes him or her to take some other action. As we have seen, the Constitution did not authorize the president to act otherwise in this case. Since the secretary of commerce had seized private property, the Court ruled against the government even though the nation's armed forces were fighting.

There have been many emergency situations, when the Supreme Court has refused to rule at all, preferring to leave the two political branches of government, Congress and the presidency, to settle the matter. For example, the Court refused to rule on cases that challenged the legality of the Vietnam War on the grounds that Congress had not declared war. Similarly, lower courts declined to rule on cases that would have prevented President George Bush from sending American soldiers to the Persian Gulf to fight Iraq in defense of Kuwait.

The President and the Political Arena

Because the courts sometimes take no position on the president's role in dealing with national security issues, most questions about it are left to be settled in the political arena. The president often has the upper hand in such cases. Why? First, the American public looks to the president to define national security threats and to say what action should and must be taken to meet them. Therefore, when the president's response is clear and firm, the public almost always supports it. Second, the president has an advantage because members of Congress do not wish to open themselves to the charge that they tied the president's hands and prevented what he asserted was action necessary to protect national security. Therefore, in the end, Congress goes along with the president, even when this seems to intrude on Congress's constitutional powers by leading the nation into war.

When the Cold War ended, Americans once again began to debate the question of what kind of emergency powers are required to meet the country's security needs and how to apply those powers in a way in keeping with the Constitution. Those who stress presidential powers have a favorite saying: "the Constitution is not a suicide pact." By this they mean that the Constitution's highest goal is to preserve the United States. Certainly, this is true. But it is also the case that claims of national security cannot be permitted to override all other considerations. Nor should they allow the president to ignore Congress's constitutional role or individual rights. Each generation of Americans needs to create its own balance anew.

ARTICLE I—The War Power; ARTICLE II—Presidential Emergency Powers; Steel Seizure Case; FIRST AMENDMENT—Freedom of the Press: Prior Restraints

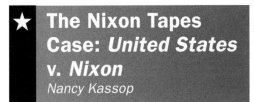

The Nixon Tapes Case: *United States v. Nixon*
Nancy Kassop

authority the power to grant legal allowance

absolute complete, pure, free from restriction or limitation

executive privilege a right granted as a benefit or advantage to officials in the executive branch of government

indictment a formal written statement charging a person or persons with an offense after a grand jury has examined the evidence and found that there is a valid case

In *United States* v. *Nixon* (1974), the Supreme Court considered whether a president may claim constitutional authority to refuse to submit documents for use as evidence to a prosecutor in charge of a criminal investigation, when there is a federal court order to do so. President Nixon maintained that Article II of the Constitution granted him an absolute "executive privilege" to protect the confidentiality of his private conversations with his White House aides.

The Supreme Court, in an 8-to-0 decision, disagreed. It ordered President Nixon to submit tape recordings of these conversations to the special prosecutor. The Court acknowledged that a president may claim executive privilege when confidentiality is needed for "the effective discharge of a President's powers" or the protection of "military, diplomatic, or sensitive security secrets." The Court held that neither situation was present in this case. Sixteen days after the Court's decision, President Nixon resigned from office—the first and only president ever to do so.

The Watergate Scandal

The case grew out of the series of events known as Watergate. It began in June 1972 with a burglary of the headquarters of the Democratic National Committee at the Watergate Hotel in Washington, D.C. Testimony at Senate hearings in June 1973 revealed that (1) officials in President Nixon's administration and in his 1972 reelection campaign committee had been involved in the plotting and cover-up of the Watergate break-in; and (2) President Nixon had employed a tape recording system in the White House Oval Office. Upon the indictment of two of

▲ "Nixon in Tape Web"
by Robert Pryor

presumptive privilege a right or immunity that is assumed to be probable, granted as a benefit or advantage of holding an office

immunity protection from legal action

the president's closest aides, H. R. Haldeman and John Ehrlichman, and of his campaign manager and former Attorney General, John Mitchell, a court battle began. The Office of the Special Prosecutor sought access to the tapes to prove that these officials had been involved. The president refused to honor a federal court order to give up the tapes, claiming that he was not subject to a court order, and that executive privilege protected his tapes from disclosure.

The President's Argument

The president based his argument on two grounds, one practical and the other constitutional. The practical argument was that he had a need to keep conversations with government officials private in order to ensure that they could advise him with complete openness. The constitutional argument was based on the independence of the executive branch to act within its own sphere. The argument rested on the doctrine of separation of powers, maintaining that a president should not be compelled to respond to a judicial subpoena in a criminal prosecution.

The Court's Decision

Chief Justice Warren Burger, appointed to the Court by President Nixon, answered these arguments in his opinion for the Court. He agreed that there was a **presumptive privilege** for presidential communications that "can be said to derive from the supremacy of each branch within its own assigned area of constitutional duties." This "is fundamental to the operation of Government and inextricably rooted in the separation of powers under the Constitution," the Chief Justice wrote. But he denied that President Nixon's broad, sweeping claim of the president to a generalized, absolute privilege should prevail over the Fifth and Sixth Amendment rights of defendants in a criminal proceeding. Under these rights, defendants were entitled to the benefit of all relevant and admissible evidence.

The Court weighed and balanced the president's interest against the needs of the criminal justice process and found a constitutional basis for executive privilege in the concept of separation of powers. But the Court held that the Constitution placed limits on that privilege when there were competing constitutional interests. The Court recognized that the privilege might be justified when it related to a president's official duties or to the delicate needs of national security. In such cases, a president might claim confidentiality. But the Court would not accept the president's claim of absolute **immunity** from the judicial process when it invaded the workings of that process.

Nixon's Resignation

United States v. *Nixon* was important for many reasons. First, it spurred President Nixon to resign from office. The Court's July 24, 1974 decision made clear that Nixon was required to turn over the tapes, although there was some question as to whether he would do so. Twelve days later, he

impeachment method by which the House of Representatives may charge the nation's highest-ranking officials, including the president, with wrongdoing; following impeachment, if the officials are found guilty of the charges, the Senate then may try them and remove them from office

demagogue leader who uses popular prejudices, and false claims and promises in order to gain power

Richard M. Nixon (1913–1994) served as a congressman and senator from California and as vice president from 1952 to 1960. In 1960 he lost a close presidential election to John F. Kennedy. Nixon was elected president in 1968. As a politician he could be a **demagogue** and he often found dealing with people difficult, but he had a penetrating mind and as a statesman he could be bold. Courts found many of his and his administration's actions to be unconstitutional. The Watergate affair, a series of scandals involving his reelection in 1972 and their cover-up, led to his resignation in August 1974. He was about to be impeached by the House and conviction by the Senate would almost certainly follow. Earlier, he had said, "I am not a crook."

implied assumed or suggested without being specifically stated

see also

ARTICLE I—The Impeachment Power;
ARTICLE II—The Executive Branch;
ARTICLE III—Establishment of Judicial
Review: *Marbury* v. *Madison*

began to release some of the tapes. These provided undeniable evidence that Nixon had had discussions about the cover-up of the Watergate burglary. An impeachment inquiry was already underway in the House of Representatives, and the information on the tapes was sufficiently damaging to the president to make the likelihood of impeachment certain. Nixon announced his resignation on August 8, effective the following day.

What the Case Means

The Court's decision was actually quite narrow. A president's wish to protect information needed for the criminal trial of his top aides is a situation that seldom occurs. But the ruling recognized for the first time an implied power of the president under Article II and the concept of separation of powers to claim executive privilege under limited conditions. The establishment of a balancing test to judge the merits of a president's claim against a competing constitutional interest is a standard to be applied to future claims. The deference the Court gave to the need for the confidentiality of information for national security purposes suggests a willingness by the Court to accept such presidential requests. The upholding of an executive privilege claim by former President Ronald Reagan at the trial of Iran–Contra defendant Admiral John Poindexter in 1990 exemplifies such willingness.

Perhaps the most important legacy of the decision was that it demonstrated that the courts can review a president's claims of power and that such claims cannot be left to the sole judgment of the president. In its opinion, the Court reaffirmed the words from *Marbury* v. *Madison* that "it is emphatically the province and duty of the judicial department to say what the law is."

▶ President Richard M. Nixon makes a speech while sitting beside the edited transcripts of the Watergate tapes.

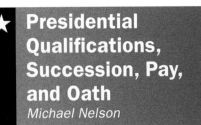

Presidential Qualifications, Succession, Pay, and Oath
Michael Nelson

affirmation declaration under the penalty of perjury

electoral college a body of people chosen by the voters in each state that selects the president and vice president of the United States

Clause 5. No person except a natural-born Citizen, or a Citizen of the United States, at the time of the Adoption of this Constitution, shall be eligible to the Office of President; neither shall any Person be eligible to that Office who shall not have attained to the Age of thirty-five years, and have been fourteen Years a Resident within the United States.

Clause 6. In Case of Removal of the President from Office, or of his Death, Resignation, or Inability to discharge the Duties of the said Office, the same shall devolve on the Vice President, and the Congress may by Law provide for the Case of Removal, Death, Resignation, or Inability, both of the President and Vice President, declaring what Officer shall then act as President, and such Officer shall act accordingly, until the disability be removed, or a President shall be elected.

Clause 7. The President shall, at stated Times, receive for his Services a Compensation, which shall neither be increased nor diminished during the Period for which he shall have been elected, and he shall not receive within that Period any other Emolument from the United States, or any of them.

*Clause 8. Before he enter on the execution of his Office, he shall take the following Oath or **Affirmation**:—"I do solemnly swear (or affirm) that I will faithfully execute the Office of President of the United States, and will, to the best of my Ability, preserve, protect, and defend the Constitution of the United States."*

After explaining in considerable detail how the president is to be selected, Article II, Section 1, of the Constitution concludes with four clauses dealing mostly with choosing the president. The first describes the qualifications necessary to be eligible for the presidency. The second clause states the order in which other officials would succeed to the presidency should the office become vacant before the president's four-year term expires. The next clause deals with the pay the chief executive receives. And the last has the oath that the president takes before he assumes office.

Qualifications Set by the Framers

The clauses detailing the presidential qualifications as well as the clauses setting up the electoral college were adopted late in the Constitutional Convention, on September 7, 1787. The two issues of how the president was to be elected and whether the Constitution should state qualifications for this office were closely connected.

Before they agreed about the electoral college, the Framers had provided for the president to be chosen by Congress, a body whose members already had met the constitutional requirements of age, residence, and citizenship. Later, the electoral college replaced Congress in choosing the president. Since there were no constitutionally stated qualifications for the members of the electoral college, the Framers decided that qualifications needed to be established for the president. This decision reflected a principle that the Framers seemed to have followed throughout the Constitutional Convention: that qualifications for an office needed to be established only if no qualifications were spelled out for those who were to elect the person to fill that office.

The delegates to the Constitutional Convention had earlier decided not to include two requirements common in state constitutions for the office of governor: a property qualification and a religious qualification. Most delegates favored the idea that the president should be a substantial property owner, but they could not agree on the details of such a requirement. The religious qualification, which the Framers opposed, reflected common practice. Thus, Article VI barred a religious test for any officeholder in the new federal government.

The Age Qualification

Just as they had done for members of Congress, the Framers established three qualifications for president: age, residency, and citizenship. In each case, the presidential qualification was higher than those for members of Congress. For example, the president was required to be at least thirty-five years old, compared to thirty years for senators and twenty-five for representatives. In each case, the Framers carefully considered their reasons for establishing these different age requirements. They believed that setting the president's age qualification at thirty-five served two purposes. One was that a higher age requirement would help to ensure that the person elected president was mature; and the second was that it would give the candidate time to achieve a public record for the voters to judge. As John Jay wrote in *The Federalist*, No. 64, this age requirement meant that "the people . . . will not be deceived by those brilliant appearances of genius and patriotism, which like transient [quickly moving] meteors, sometimes mislead as well as dazzle."

▶ Supreme Court Justice William Rehnquist administers oath of office at the 1993 inauguration of President Bill Clinton.

The Residency Qualification

The other qualifications—that the president must be at least "fourteen years a resident within the United States" and a "natural-born citizen"— were based less on principle than on the concerns of the moment. The residency requirement was designed mainly to eliminate from consideration both Tories—those Americans who had supported the British during the Revolution, many of whom had fled to England—and popular foreign military leaders such as Baron von Steuben of Prussia, who had come to the United States and became a general in the American forces.

The Natural-born Citizen Qualification

The Framers included the natural-born citizen requirement to end the rumors spread during the Philadelphia convention that they were plotting to invite a European prince to rule the United States. (King George III's second son, Frederick, Duke of York, was one widely rumored choice.) The Framers, of course, had no such plan. Yet they were aware that establishing a powerful, independent presidency would provoke those who opposed this idea to charge that the president could become as powerful as a monarch. Therefore, the Framers decided to include the citizenship requirement. Unfortunately, the meaning of "natural-born citizen" was unclear then, and it remains so. Does it refer to persons born on American soil, or to persons born to American parents?

Presidential Succession

impeach to set up a formal hearing on charges of high crimes and misdemeanors

The Framers' treatment of presidential succession left many questions unanswered. This provision, like most of the others in Article II, Section 1, was not resolved until the Constitutional Convention's final days. It provided that if the president died, resigned, was impeached and convicted, or was unable to "discharge the powers and duties of the said office, the same shall devolve on the vice president." The wording of this clause left its meaning unclear. Did "the same" refer to "the said office" (the presidency)? Or did it refer only to its "powers and duties"? The Framers seem to have intended the second meaning, that the vice president was supposed to become, in effect, an acting president until a special election could be called to choose a new chief executive. But they did not make their meaning clear. This left open the possibility that the vice president would not just assume the powers and duties of the presidency temporarily, but actually would become president and serve out the remainder of the four-year term.

In 1841, Vice President John Tyler acted decisively to take advantage of this possibility. President William Henry Harrison had died just one month after his inauguration, the first president ever not to complete his term. Tyler succeeded him and declared that he was now president for the next three years and eleven months. Later vice presidents followed Tyler's precedent, which eventually was made part of the Constitution in the Twenty-fifth Amendment in 1967. This amendment also treated the troubling question of how succession to the presidency was to occur if the president became disabled. The Constitutional Convention's original handling of the matter was so inadequate that one delegate, John Dickinson of Pennsylvania asked, "What is the extent of the term 'disability' and who is to be the judge of it?" No delegate answered the question.

In the matter of presidential succession, the Framers also charged Congress with enacting a law to create a line of succession extending beyond the vice president. Congress did so in 1792, by requiring that if both the presidential and vice presidential offices were vacant at the same time, a special election would be held. In the meantime, the **president** *pro tempore* of the Senate, who is usually its senior member, would serve as acting president. This act was replaced in 1886 by a new law placing the line of succession in the president's cabinet. The succession would follow the order in which the executive departments were created, beginning with the secretary of state. In 1947, Congress passed a revised version of the 1792 act. This version replaced the line of succession with the Speaker of the House first, the president of the Senate second, and cabinet members third. A special election no longer was required.

Fortunately, there has never been a vacancy in both the presidency and vice presidency at the same time. This is truly remarkable, because nine vice presidents have succeeded to the presidency, and nine others have died or resigned while serving as vice president. Even so, a double vacancy that would invoke any of the succession laws has never occurred. The Twenty-fifth Amendment has dramatically reduced the likelihood of such a double vacancy by providing for the appointment of a new vice president when a vacancy occurs in that office.

president *pro tempore* (Latin, "for the time being") serving as president on a temporary basis

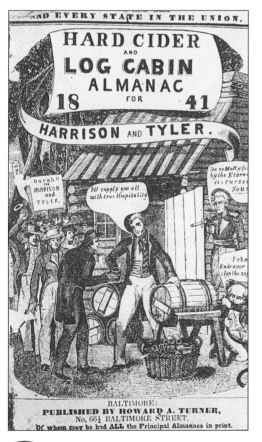

▲ The cover of the Hard Cider and Log Cabin Almanac of 1841 showing presidential candidate William Henry Harrison and his running mate, John Tyler. The ticket won the election of 1840, but Harrison died in office after just one month, leaving Tyler to succeed him.

The President's Salary

The Framers included in Article II, Section I, Clause 7, a provision that "the president shall, at stated times, receive for his services, a compensation." Benjamin Franklin objected to this provision at the Constitutional Convention because it would unite two unworthy "passions" in one office, "the love of power, and the love of money," but his objection was ignored. In later years, Congress has enacted laws that have raised the president's salary from $25,000 in 1789 to $50,000 in 1873, to $75,000 in 1909, and to $100,000, plus an expense account of $50,000, in 1949. Another increase, voted into law by Congress in 1969, raised the president's salary to $200,000, plus a $50,000 expense account.

Most important to the delegates at the Philadelphia convention was the provision that the president's salary "shall neither be increased nor diminished during the period for which he shall have been elected." This means that when Congress raises the president's salary, the raise does not take effect until the next president is inaugurated. The delegates felt very strongly that Congress should not be able to use money as a tool to influence the president, whether by raising the salary of a president it likes or by cutting the salary of a president it dislikes. To make this even less possible, the delegates also provided that the president "shall not receive any other emolument [compensation] from the United States, or any of them."

The President's Oath

The final provision in Article II, Section 1, is the president's oath of office. Phrases from the oath have become familiar to Americans, who have heard them recited every four years, at noon on the January 20th that follows each presidential election: "I do solemnly swear," "faithfully execute the office of president," and "preserve, protect, and defend the Constitution." By tradition, presidents since George Washington have added "so help me God" at the end of the oath, although this phrase does not appear in the Constitution.

Although Article VI states that all legislators, judges, and officials of both the national and various state governments "shall be bound by oath or affirmation, to support this Constitution," the president's oath is the only oath of office spelled out in the Constitution. This has led some presidents, including Abraham Lincoln at the beginning of the Civil War, to act on the understanding that presidents have powers to uphold the Constitution beyond those specifically stated there.

ments entered into in the case of Korea, or in any other military activity. The procedure adopted by Congress in the UN Participation Act to safeguard legislative prerogatives had lost its force.

The Watergate affair was a series of scandals involving President Richard Nixon. It started in July of 1972, when agents of Nixon's reelection committee were arrested in Democratic Party Headquarters, in the Watergate apartment building in Washington, D.C. after an attempt to tap telephones there. Senate hearings revealed that Nixon had taped conversations in the Oval Office. In October of 1973, Archibald Cox, the special prosecutor appointed to investigate the affair, requested these tapes. He threatened to secure a judicial ruling that Nixon was violating a court order to run tapes over to a federal judge. Nixon ordered Attorney General Eliot Richardson to fire Cox. Richardson refused and resigned. So did his deputy, William Ruckelshaus. The third-ranking Justice Department official, Solicitor General Robert Bork, who represented the administration before the Supreme Court, finally agreed to fire Cox.

The White House announcement of the resignations and firing led to instantaneous demonstrations in Washington—the "Saturday Night Massacre," as it quickly came to be called. Cars honked outside the White House as protesters held up signs saying "Honk for Impeachment." Television specials spread the shock nationwide. Western Union announced it had proceeded "the heaviest concentrated volume (of telegrams) on record"— 450,000 within ten days. Nixon's fellow Republicans were as vehement as Democrats. Cox's successor, Leon Jaworski, succeeded in getting the tapes, and subsequently he convicted several high-ranking administration officials.

ARTICLE II—The Executive Branch;
TWENTY-FIFTH AMENDMENT

Commander-in-Chief
Louis Fisher

militia a part-time army made up of ordinary citizens

impeachment method by which the House of Representatives may charge the nation's highest-ranking officials, including the president, with wrongdoing; following impeachment, if the officials are found guilty of the charges, the Senate then may try them and remove them from office

authority the power to grant legal allowance
waive give up voluntarily

vest to grant with particular authority, property, and rights

ARTICLE II, SECTION 1, CLAUSE 1, OF THE CONSTITUTION STATES

*The President shall be Commander in Chief of the Army and Navy of the United States, and of the **Militia** of the several States, when called into actual Service of the United States; he may require the Opinion, in writing, of the principal Officer in each of the executive Departments, upon any subject relating to the Duties of their respective Offices, and he shall have the power to grant Reprieves and Pardons for Offenses against the United States, except in Cases of **Impeachment**.*

The Framers of the Constitution placed the responsibility to serve as commander-in-chief upon the president. Article II, Section 2, Clause 1 provides that the president "shall be commander in chief of the army and navy of the United States and of the militia of the several states, when called into the actual service of the United States." The scope of that power has been debated ever since. Does this constitutional provision merely confer a title on the president, or does it carry with it additional powers and duties?

The Steel Seizure Case

In the Supreme Court's decision in *Youngstown Sheet & Tube Co.* v. *Sawyer* (1952), Justice Robert Jackson, in his concurring opinion, concluded that the commander-in-chief clause implies "something more than an empty title. But just what authority goes with the name has plagued presidential advisers who would not waive or narrow it by nonassertion yet cannot say where it begins or ends." He observed that the commander-in-chief clause is sometimes advanced to support "any presidential action, internal or external, involving use of force, the idea being that it vests power to do anything, anywhere, that can be done with an army or navy." But Justice Jackson rejected such ambitious claims, remarking that nothing would be "more sinister and alarming than that a President whose conduct of foreign affairs is so largely uncontrolled, and often even is unknown, can vastly enlarge his mastery over the internal affairs of the country by his own commitment of the Nation's armed forces to some foreign venture."

Significance of the Clause

Making the president the commander-in-chief of the armed forces protects several important principles. One is unity of command. As Alexander Hamilton explained in *The Federalist*, No. 74, leading forces in wartime "most peculiarly demands those qualities which distinguish the exercise of power by a single head." The power of directing war "forms a usual and essential part of the definition of the executive authority."

A second important principle is the supremacy of civilian authority over the military. The Framers wanted the leader of the nation's armed forces to be a civilian president, not a military officer. In the Declaration of Independence, one of the many charges of abuse listed against King George III was that he had "affected to render [caused to make] the Military independent of and superior to the Civil Power." In 1861, Attorney General Edward Bates explained that the president is commander-in-chief not because he is "skilled in the art of war and qualified to marshal a host [arrange a director or general] in the field of battle." Instead, the president preserves the principle of civilian supremacy. Whenever officers lead armed forces against an enemy, they are "subject to the orders of the civil magistrate."

Powers of the Commander-in-chief

In *The Federalist*, No. 69, Alexander Hamilton claimed that the office of commander-in-chief "would amount to nothing more than the **supreme** command and direction of the military and naval forces, as first general and admiral of the Confederacy" (that is, the original thirteen United States). His description proved accurate in the case of some presidents, while others have asserted greater authority, using their power to initiate war and expand military conflicts.

supreme having the highest authority

Jefferson's take. President Thomas Jefferson agreed that the powers of the commander-in-chief were limited to defensive military actions. In his first annual message to Congress, on December 8, 1801, Jefferson described the actions he was taking against the Barbary pirates who had demanded bribes to permit American vessels to sail in the Mediterranean Sea. Jefferson had sent ships to protect American ships there against threatened attacks. He then asked Congress for its advice on further actions, stating that he was "[u]nauthorized by the Constitution, without the sanction of Congress, to go beyond the line of defense." It was up to Congress to authorize "measures for offense also," because such actions were "confided by the Constitution to the Legislature exclusively."

President Polk's interpretation. Yet President James Polk's actions showed what choices are available to a president who has a standing army to direct. In 1846, he ordered General Zachary Taylor to occupy disputed territory along the Texas-Mexican border. After fighting broke out between American and Mexican soldiers, Polk told Congress that "war exists." Although Congress declared war against Mexico, in 1848 the House of Representatives censured Polk's action, claiming that the war had been "unnecessarily and unconstitutionally begun by the President of the United States."

Illustration of the sinking of the U.S. frigate Philadelphia, which President Jefferson had sent to the Mediterranean in an effort to protect American ships from Barbary pirate raids.

President Lincoln's approach. In April 1861, while Congress was in recess, President Abraham Lincoln issued proclamations calling up the state militia, suspending the **writ of habeas corpus** and placing a blockade on the rebellious Southern states. In *The Prize Cases* (1863), Justice Robert Grier wrote for the Supreme Court that the president as commander-in-chief "has no power to initiate or declare a war either against a foreign nation or a domestic State." But in the case of a foreign

writ of habeas corpus (Latin, "produce the body") a court command to produce the person being held in order to determine whether the person's detention is lawful; a way of making sure that a criminal trial has been fair

invasion, the president not only was authorized "but bound to resist force by force. He does not initiate the war, but is bound to accept the challenge without waiting for any special legislative authority."

President Lincoln was unsure whether he had constitutional authority to act as he did. When Congress returned from its recess, he said that his actions "whether strictly legal or not, were ventured upon under what appeared to be a popular demand and a public necessity, trusting then, as now, that Congress would readily ratify them." Congress passed legislation "approving, legalizing, and making valid all the acts, proclamations, and orders of the President, etc., as if they had been issued and done under the previous express authority and direction of the Congress of the United States."

International Engagements

Congress made formal declarations of war in the Spanish-American War of 1898 and in World Wars I and II. In the case of the two world wars, Presidents Woodrow Wilson and Franklin D. Roosevelt took a number of independent actions that pushed the United States toward those conflicts. They did so despite the fact that in the elections immediately preceding the wars, they promised voters that American soldiers would not be involved. On October 31, 1916, President Wilson announced: "I am not expecting this country to get into war." On October 30, 1940, President Roosevelt told a crowd: "I have said this before, but I shall say it again and again and again: 'Your boys are not going to be sent into any foreign war.'"

In both world wars, the United States fought alongside allies. The likelihood of future American involvement in international crises increased with the signing of the United Nations Charter in 1945. Under Article 41 of the Charter, the Security Council may decide to recommend "measures not involving the use of armed force" to deal with any threat to the peace, breach of the peace, or act of aggression.

The charter's provisions. If these measures turn out to be ineffective, Article 43 provides that all members of the United Nations shall undertake to make available to the Security Council, "on its call and in accordance with a special agreement or agreements," armed forces and other assistance. These agreements spell out the numbers and types of armed forces, their degree of readiness and general location, and the nature of the assistance to be provided. Article 43 further states that the special agreements shall be ratified by each nation "in accordance with their respective constitutional processes."

The United Nations Participation Act. The steps set forth in Article 43 of the UN Charter raised the possibility of substantial presidential power, depending on the meaning of "constitutional processes." To prevent possible abuse of power by the president, Congress passed the United Nations Participation Act in 1945, requiring that these special agreements "shall be subject to the approval of the Congress by appropriate Act or joint resolution." Under this Act, the president could commit American armed forces to the United Nations only after Congress granted its approval.

---

ratify to formally approve a document, thereby making it legal

legislation the exercise of the power and function of making laws

---

Throughout most of American history, the term "commander-in-chief" meant only that the president was the highest officer in the armed forces. Franklin D. Roosevelt expanded the concept during World War II. He realized, however, that in important ways he was still subject to Congress, and almost without exception he made certain to get Congress's approval on matters not dealing specifically with the theater of war. "When the war is won," FDR said, "the powers under which I act automatically revert to the people— to whom they belong." He chose the leading military commanders, including Dwight Eisenhower, who led the Allies' forces in Europe. Roosevelt was also intimately involved in developing military strategy, and approved its broad design before it was put into effect.

The Korean crisis. Nevertheless, on June 27, 1950, President Harry Truman announced to the nation that the Security Council had called upon all members of the United Nations to provide assistance for its resolution ordering North Korea to end hostilities against South Korea and withdraw its forces to the 38th Parallel. Truman ordered American air and sea forces to help South Korea defend itself, and called the military conflict in Korea a "United Nations police action." Yet he never asked Congress for authority to take such action. Nor were special UN agreements entered into in the case of Korea, or in any other military activity. The procedure adopted by Congress in the UN Participation Act to safeguard legislative prerogatives had lost its force.

Vietnam

President Truman also provided substantial military and economic assistance to the French fighting in Indochina. President Dwight D. Eisenhower continued this policy, committing the first American troops, a force of 200, to Southeast Asia. After the French surrendered in 1954, Vietnam was divided between north and south. Then President John F. Kennedy increased the number of American military advisers in Vietnam from 700 to 16,000.

During the 1964 election campaign, President Lyndon B. Johnson promised that he was "not about to send American boys 9[,000] or 10,000 miles away from home to do what Asian boys ought to be doing for themselves." Yet in February 1965, Johnson ordered large numbers of American bombing missions, followed by the commitment of more than 500,000 American troops to Vietnam. President Richard M. Nixon, elected in 1968 to end the war, extended it into Laos and Cambodia.

By denying funds for all combat activities in Southeast Asia in 1973, Congress finally ended American involvement in the Vietnam War. In that same year, Congress also passed the War Powers Resolution, designed to limit presidential power and ensure congressional control of military action. This statute had some success during the next ten to fifteen years, but presidential power gradually widened. In 1995, in a vote in the House of Representatives, members came close to repealing the War Powers Resolution.

President Bush and the Persian Gulf Operation

On August 2, 1990, Iraqi leader Saddam Hussein sent an invasion force into Kuwait. President George Bush, in a defensive move, sent American troops to Saudi Arabia. After doubling the size of the American forces in the Middle East by November, he had the military power needed to wage an **offensive** war. Instead of seeking authority from Congress, he forged an international alliance and encouraged the UN Security Council to authorize the use of force against Iraq. Bush administration officials testified that there was no need to obtain "additional authorization" from Congress. Yet Bush eventually asked Congress for support. Congress

offensive marked by aggressive action, that is initiated rather than defensive

President Bill Clinton addresses U.S. troops participating in United Nations operations in Bosnia (1996).

statutory legal

see also

ARTICLE I—The War Power; ARTICLE II— National Security and the Presidency; Presidential Emergency Powers; Steel Seizure Case; Writ of Habeas Corpus

prerogative having to do with a special right or privilege particular to an office

enacted legislation on January 12, 1991, authorizing the president to take offensive action against Iraq.

President Clinton's Use of Military Forces

Like Presidents Truman and Bush, President Bill Clinton argued that he could use military force against other nations without seeking authority from Congress.

The crisis in Haiti. In October 1993, Clinton threatened to use American military forces to restore Jean-Bertrand Aristide to power as president of Haiti. Congress debated legislation that would limit Clinton's power to send troops to Haiti unless Congress specifically authorized it, but never passed binding laws on this issue.

On July 31, 1994, the UN Security Council adopted a resolution "inviting" all nations, particularly those in the region of Haiti, to use "all necessary means" to put Aristide back in power. Two months later, Clinton told the American public that he was prepared to use military force to invade Haiti, referring to the UN resolution and the need to "carry out the will of the United Nations." He did not seek authority from Congress. But an American invasion became unnecessary when former President Jimmy Carter negotiated an agreement in which the military leaders in Haiti agreed to step down and to permit Aristide's return.

Conflict in the Balkans. When Clinton considered the use of American air and ground forces in Bosnia, Congress considered various statutory restrictions on such presidential military initiatives. Clinton declared that he would "strenuously oppose" any attempt to limit his foreign policy powers. In 1994, he began to authorize air strikes in Bosnia, relying on his powers as commander-in-chief as well as various UN resolutions and decisions by the United States' North Atlantic Treaty Organization (NATO) allies. Air strikes continued in 1995.

After Clinton proposed to send American ground forces into Bosnia, both houses of Congress drafted legislation to restrict his actions unless he first obtained congressional authorization. But those proposals were never enacted. Clinton sent 20,000 American troops to Bosnia. On December 21, 1995, Clinton announced that he expected this military mission to Bosnia to last about a year. On December 17, 1996, he extended the stay of American forces there for another eighteen months. In late 1997, he said that he expected American troops to remain in Bosnia for an additional year.

Conclusion

The Framers assumed that in a system of government based on separation of powers, each branch would protect its prerogatives by fighting off attempts to encroach on them. That idea seemed to work well for the war power during the first century and a half of the nation's history. But since 1950, the record has been one of presidents asserting increasing power without congressional resistance.

Index to Volume 1